CAMBRIDGE LIBRARY COLLECTION

Books of enduring scholarly value

Printing and Publishing History

The interface between authors and their readers is a fascinating subject in its own right, revealing a great deal about social attitudes, technological progress, aesthetic values, fashionable interests, political positions, economic constraints, and individual personalities. This part of the Cambridge Library Collection reissues classic studies in the area of printing and publishing history that shed light on developments in typography and book design, printing and binding, the rise and fall of publishing houses and periodicals, and the roles of authors and illustrators. It documents the ebb and flow of the book trade supplying a wide range of customers with products from almanacs to novels, bibles to erotica, and poetry to statistics.

Bibliophobia

In 1809, Thomas Frognall Dibdin (1776–1847) published the first edition of *Bibliomania*, focussing on the contemporary craze for book collecting. Introduced in English at the end of the eighteenth century, the term 'bibliomania' – or 'book-madness' – gained popularity with the publication of Dibdin's book, in which bibliophiles conduct dialogues on the nature and history of book collecting, and the symptoms of and possible remedies for this 'fatal disease'. Published in 1832 under the pseudonym Mercurius Rusticus, *Bibliophobia* is a short pamphlet, which presents itself as a letter to the author of *Bibliomania*. The narrator, a book-lover himself, goes on a 'bibliopolistic pilgrimage', only to find out that 'bibliomania is no more', and that 'books are only the shadow of what they were'. From book-lovers to collectors, and from booksellers to libraries, the narrator carries out his entertaining yet melancholic investigation all the way to the Bodleian Library.

T0382607

Cambridge University Press has long been a pioneer in the reissuing of out-of-print titles from its own backlist, producing digital reprints of books that are still sought after by scholars and students but could not be reprinted economically using traditional technology. The Cambridge Library Collection extends this activity to a wider range of books which are still of importance to researchers and professionals, either for the source material they contain, or as landmarks in the history of their academic discipline.

Drawing from the world-renowned collections in the Cambridge University Library, and guided by the advice of experts in each subject area, Cambridge University Press is using state-of-the-art scanning machines in its own Printing House to capture the content of each book selected for inclusion. The files are processed to give a consistently clear, crisp image, and the books finished to the high quality standard for which the Press is recognised around the world. The latest print-on-demand technology ensures that the books will remain available indefinitely, and that orders for single or multiple copies can quickly be supplied.

The Cambridge Library Collection will bring back to life books of enduring scholarly value (including out-of-copyright works originally issued by other publishers) across a wide range of disciplines in the humanities and social sciences and in science and technology.

Bibliophobia

Remarks on the Present Languid and Depressed State of Literature and the Book Trade.

In a Letter Addressed to the Author of the Bibliomania

THOMAS FROGNALL DIBDIN

CAMBRIDGE
UNIVERSITY PRESS

CAMBRIDGE UNIVERSITY PRESS

Cambridge, New York, Melbourne, Madrid, Cape Town, Singapore,
São Paolo, Delhi, Dubai, Tokyo

Published in the United States of America by Cambridge University Press, New York

www.cambridge.org
Information on this title: www.cambridge.org/9781108015592

© in this compilation Cambridge University Press 2010

This edition first published 1932
This digitally printed version 2010

ISBN 978-1-108-01559-2 Paperback

BIBLIOPHOBIA.

REMARKS

ON THE

PRESENT LANGUID AND DEPRESSED STATE OF

LITERATURE

AND THE BOOK TRADE.

IN A LETTER

ADDRESSED TO THE AUTHOR OF THE

𝔅𝔦𝔟𝔩𝔦𝔬𝔪𝔞𝔫𝔦𝔞.

BY

MERCURIUS RUSTICUS.

———

WITH NOTES

BY CATO PARVUS.

———

" FEAR is the order of the day. To those very natural and long established fears of bailiffs and taxgatherers, must now be added the fear of *Reform*, of *Cholera*, and of BOOKS." p. 6.

LONDON:

HENRY BOHN, 4, YORK STREET, COVENT GARDEN.

———

1832.

ADVERTISEMENT.

The ensuing pages would never have seen the light, but that, on shewing them in MS. to a neighbouring friend—who lives just across the moor—he was pleased to express a very favourable opinion of their probable good tendency, if given to the world; adding, that a few NOTES,* *which he would cheerfully supply, might perhaps help to promote the object in view. As I knew him to be well versed in the arcana both of black-letter and of modern publications, and most regular in his annual visits to the Metropolis, I thankfully accepted his offer. I hope therefore that the text and notes together may prove acceptable to the kind-hearted reader, who cannot but sympathize with their author in the present melancholy prevalence of the disease of* Bibliophobia; *which is altogether new in its characteristics, and ominous of the most direful results.*

The first two notes of my friend bear his name: CATO PARVUS, or the Initials: afterwards, they have neither name nor initials. My own few notes bear the initials M. R.

A LETTER, &c.

Laurel Lodge.
Oct. 31, 1831.

REVEREND SIR,

It is now, I believe, upwards of twenty-years, since you kindly undertook the useful task of making the public acquainted with the symptoms or characteristics of the dreadful disease called the BIBLIOMANIA. With the symptoms of the disease, you also furnished them with the means of its cure. But, strange to say, the very opposite to the effect predicted took place. The mania increased in fury. Its ravages spread far and wide, and its victims were numerous. Men seemed to judge by " the rule of contrary." They hunted hole and corner for *black letter*, and *large paper*, and *uncut*, copies of the several works they were in search of; and, with the palpable evidence of astounding facts before their eyes, they rushed infatuatedly forward to embrace the very causes of self-destruction. Such heart-rending cases of *felo-de-se* had never been before recorded.

Things are strangely altered of late: and passions and tastes have taken a very opposite tone. Objects, which formerly rivetted attention, and begat attachment, are now considered almost as those of horror and alarm. In short, FEAR is the order of the day. To those very natural and long-established fears of bailiffs and tax-gatherers, must now be added the fear of *Reform*, of *Cholera*, and of BOOKS.

I am induced to trouble you with a few remarks upon this melancholy but highly interesting subject, in consequence of a visit recently paid to a friend in town; whom, in the "good old times" of Bibliomania, I used to accompany to book-sales:—from whom I learned to "hit my bird" with unerring dexterity, and, in consequence, to store my larder with a profusion of game. In other words, to make my book-purchases with discrimination, and to enrich my shelves with a due sprinkling of choice copies. I staid with my friend during the three latter months of "the season," as it is called; and when I returned to my solitary rural residence, and cast an eager look over those "precious gems," which, in former times, seemed to sparkle with unrivalled lustre, somehow or other they appeared to fall flat and dead upon my notice. Ill-humour, vexation, and wrath at the capriciousness of public taste, all united to make me retreat precipitately from my *book-room—*

for it aspires not to the dignified appellative of a
" LIBRARY." However, after a few short, heavy
breathings, I returned to my once favourite
haunt of retirement. I carried with me all my
former kind and warm-hearted feelings towards
those objects of silent but eloquent instruction;
and throwing myself into my walnut-tree curi-
ously-carved armed chair, read to myself a sharp
lecture on the absurdity of yielding to the very
feelings which I had deprecated. I then seemed
to breathe freely again: and signing a tacit con-
tract with my beloved, resolved that nothing
in future should ever cause me to bate one jot of
my attachment towards my Dugdales and my
Hearnes.

It is true—living in a village as I do—there
is little inducement from without to cause my
book-passion to increase in ardour. The Squire
has not the smallest notion of the value of large
margins or rough edges: and when I took down
the *Fructus Temporum*, printed by *Machlinia*, as
the *ne plus ultra* of my book-gems, he declared
that he had " never seen anything, in the shape
of a book, half so frightful in his life!"* The

* The Squire may be forgiven for this *brusquerie* in passing
judgment. It *is*, typographically speaking, a " frightful" book.
A good deal of puzzle belongs to the identifying of the Chro-
nicle printed in the *Abbey of St. Alban*, and of that printed by
Machlinia. See these books fully described in the *Bibl.
Spenceriana*, vol IV. 369-73; 393. CATO PARVUS.

Clergyman, in all *other* respects a most exemplary character, has no idea of the worth of my octodecimo black regiment of Latimer, Fox, and Drant ; * but obstinately adheres to his Barrow, Tillotson, and Atterbury. I pity, from my heart, such a circumscribed range of taste: and giving up the Squire as incorrigible, hope yet to teach the Vicar better things.

I confess that one of the principal motives for troubling you with this epistolary address, is, the excessive astonishment and chagrin which I experienced at the sale of the *Autograph Novels* of the renowned Author of Waverley. What, Sir, is it come to *this* ? Are the fire and spirit and emulation of our young nobility and gentry quite extinct? Is the love of legendary lore wholly defunct? Are the gewgaws of jewellery, the tawdryness of furniture, the trickery of horse dealing, the brittleness of Dresden and Sèvre ware, and " such-like," to form paramount objects of purchase and speculation, by those,

---

* Copious and curious specimens of the pulpit eloquence of Latimer, Fox, and Drant, will be found in the *Library Companion*, p. 66-81 ; to which add, as there adduced, specimens from a contemporary of the name of Edgeworth. When I quote from the Library Companion, I wish it to be understood that I quote from the first, or as some booksellers call it, the *Breeches Edition* of 1824. The *second* is however the more valuable. Will posterity ever be made acquainted with the mystery belonging to this *small-clothes* designation ? C. P.

whose purses are usually well lined with pis-
toles? In what an age of effeminacy among men,
and of utter nonchalance and apathy among wo-
men, do we now live! At the sale in question,
scarcely " Three Gentlemen of Verona" were
present. Mr. Evans eyed his auditory with
evident marks of surprise and discomfort. He
expected to have found—with the Campbells and
Moors, the Galts, Bulwers, and Wards, of the
day—half-a-score of Roxburghers, with the élite
of the Athenæum, and even a due sprinkling of
the fashionable *Bas Bleu.* He found no such
thing. One or two authors, and a brace of M.P.'s
only were present. The rest were booksellers; of
whom Mr. Thorpe, as usual, occupied a good portion of the foreground: and, to his credit it must
be added, became the largest bibliopolistic purchaser on the occasion.

Conticuêre omnes intentique ora tenebant,

as Mr. Evans commenced his " prologue to the
swelling act." It was evident, however, that an
under current was running pretty strongly against
the audible tide of speech: at times, even " vox
faucibus hæsit." Still it was a good earnest ha-
rangue—well timed—and to those, who did not
remember the "oratio parainetica " preceding the
sub hastâ sale of the Valdarfer Boccaccio and the

vellum Livy of Sweynheim and Pannartz,* the
effort was creditable and effective. But oh! Sir,
what language can express the surprise of both
auctioneer and company, when the *Monastery*, the
first article in the sale, produced only the sum of
£18. 18s.!† Where were ye, ye pains-taking, fid-
dle-faddling, indefatigable collectors of Franks—
ye threaders of autographic scraps—ye *Album-ites*,
" et hoc genus omne?"—where were ye " in that

* See a very full and particular description of the sales of
these celebrated volumes in the Ninth Day of the *Bibliographical Decameron*, vol. III. pp. 62-117. A sequel, of some
interest, belongs to the narrative there disclosed. Earl
Spencer, in the year 1819, at the sale of the library of the
Marquis of Blandford, (now Duke of Marlborough,) who
had purchased the Boccaccio at the Duke of Roxburgh's sale
for £2260., became possessed of that treasure for less than half
the sum. The vellum Livy of 1469, which the late Sir M.
Sykes, Bart. purchased at the sale of Mr. Edward's library
in 1815, for £903, was purchased by Messrs. Payne and Foss,
at the sale of Sir Mark's library in 1824, for £472. 10s., and
sold by them to the late Mr. Dent for 500 guineas. At the sale
of Mr. Dent's library in 1827, this book, for the *third* time,
was disposed of by public auction, by Mr. Evans, to Messrs.
Payne and Foss, for £262. 10s. It is now—and long may it
there continue—in the very fine library of the Rt. Hon. Thos.
Grenville. Could its first English possessor have survived the
intelligence, that his DARLING LIVY would one day droop its
wings so low?

† The lots, with their respective prices, were as follows:—
1. *The Monastery*, perfect, £18. 18s: 2. *Guy Mannering*, wanting a leaf at the end of vol. 2, £27. 10s: 3. *Old Mortality*,
perfect, £33: 4. *The Antiquary*, perfect, £42: 5. *Rob Roy*,
perfect, £50: 6. *Peveril of the Peak*, perfect, £42: 7.

hour ?" One would have thought that the original drafts of those master-pieces of human wit, eloquence, and passion—struck-off by the great KNOWN UNKNOWN—would have attracted crowds of competitors within the arena of Mr. Evans's auction-room : that scarcely breathing-space, much less standing-room, would have been afforded : and that Scotland herself would have furnished champions to carry off the richer prizes at the point of the claymore!

I own, that I was bewildered with the scene before me. I was, indeed, sorrow-stricken—chop-fallen—and evidently depressed. My friend perceived it. He essayed to sooth and to cheer me : but melancholy, as black and deep as any depicted by Bright or Burton,* had taken entire possession of me. I slunk quietly behind one of the square pillars, at right and left of the rostrum, and resolved to be a mute, but not unwatchful spectator of all around me. "What" (said I to myself,) "not *one* specimen for Bodley—for the British—for the London—for the Royal—for the Advocates—for Dublin ?"† Then again for *indi-*

Waverley, imperfect, £18 : 8. *The Abbot*, imperfect, £14: 9. *Ivanhoe*, imperfect, £12 : 10. *The Pirate*, imperfect, £12: 11. *Fortunes of Nigel*, imperfect, £16. 16*s*. 12. *Kenilworth*, imperfect, £17 : 13. *Bride of Lammermoor*, only 61 pages, £14. 14*s*.

* Bright's treatise on Melancholy was first published, I believe, in 1586—Burton's, in 1621.

† I presume, for the sake of brevity, the adjunct of "Li-

vidual competitorship. Where was Mr. D. T.
and Mr. A., and Mr. U.? All asleep—as well as
far away? It should seem so; for the produce
of the whole lots did not amount to quite a *fifth*
of what was expected.*

> " Excidat ille dies ævo, neu postera credant
> Sæcula !"

It will scarcely be believed, that the spirit
evinced at the previous sale of the late Mr. Hamper's *Manuscripts*,† should have become, as if
struck by some benumbing talisman, paralised at
this. The man, whose genius had supplied such
abundant food for delightful recreation and in-

---

brary," has been purposely left out in the above designa-
tions. There is, I fear, a sad state of torpor—a chilling indifference to the genuine book-feeling—possessing many of the
guardians of the above several public repositories. How
hesitatingly, and how rarely, are purchases made!

* The fact, as I understood it, was THIS. The proprietors of the MSS. were offered by the trustees of the Advocates'
Library, £1000. for the whole. This offer was not thought
sufficiently liberal; and the proprietors stood out for another
thousand. This contre-projet was not listened to for a moment: and the hammer of Mr. Evans was in consequence to
decide the matter irrevocably. The MSS. came to town; and
the result of the entire sale of those that were put up was, as
is above stated. We know there are such things as "out-
standing one's market." The general impression was, at the
outset, that they would average £50. a lot.

† The sale of Mr. Hamper's printed books and MSS.
took place in 1831. There was a most interesting mélange:
and the last day's sale of MSS. and autographs, produced
above £1100.

struction, for the last thirty-years, had the morti-
fication to learn that the *autographic* taste of his
vaunting Southern neighbours was a mere capricious impulse—a childish and fickle conceit—
without intelligible motive or object. Giving
my friend the slip, I stole sulkily away; resolving
to bid adieu to book-sales and book-purchases, of
every description, for *one* season. This unex-
pected result expedited my departure from town ;
and I found myself at *Laurel Lodge,* a thoughtful,
disappointed inmate—when I had hoped to have
entered it with alacrity and glee. At first, I
was not only disconsolate, but absolutely peevish
and irritable. As before intimated, I seemed to
loathe my library. I even shunned society. I
sought only my alcove and sweet-briar walks;
but the blossoms had lost their hue and fragrance.
The sky was never clear. The heavens were
never blue. The throstle had learned the chatter
of the jay. The nightingale was always in C flat.

Another consideration has somewhat damped
my spirits, and helped to give the leaves of the
beech and the oak (in my lower-meadow-walk)
a premature " sere and yellow" tinge. Just before my departure from town, I made a few
book-pilgrimages from one end of it to the other.
Starting from the corner of Cornhill, where those
most respectable brothers — the *Gemini* of the
eastern hemisphere—reside, I leisurely strolled
towards St. James's Palace ; calling, as my cus-

tom ever **was,** upon several bibliopoles in my way. To begin with my start. Time was, Sir, as you know full-well, and better than myself, when more than *one* British merchant would let his carriage drop down a few paces towards the London Tavern, (for the racket and roar of the four crossing roads, or streets, put the wheels of a gentleman's carriage in great jeopardy) and its inmate would step into the shop of Messrs. J. & A. Arch—and after a little pleasant interchange of literary gossip, take down—ay, and forthwith take *up,* and away with him, into his carriage—more than one portly folio, or wide-spreading quarto. I have known a whole row of a choicely coloured *Buffon,* in the former shape—and a whole series of the *Chronicles,* in the latter shape—disposed of in a trice, by a customer, who not only knew what he was about, but who loved, as regularly as the January dividends came in, to stand square and firm upon the credit side of the booksellers' ledger.* " How comes it," quoth I, " gentlemen, that there is nothing now *stirring* in this way?— that over the gilded tops of these volumes there is a somewhat dense layer of dust? and that, across yonder set of Grævius and Gronovius, the spider hath been allowed to spin his subtle web?" The answer was prompt, and too well founded. " Bib-

---

* The late Mr. Rennie used to say—" I am upon good terms with all the booksellers, and there is one thing for which they *ought* to like me—I never go to a *Sale* for any thing that I can get at a *shop.*" M. R.

liomania was no more. The canons of Dr. Dibdin were no longer assented to. A frightful heresy was abroad. The wished for *Reform in Parliament*, like Aaron's serpent, had swallowed up every other interest and pursuit; and books were now only the shadow of what they were. However, let but a *perfect Coverdale's Bible* turn up, and we shall see whether the strong box cannot afford a *settler*—to the tune of £100.—for its acquisition!"

The *Row* was the next quarter to be visited : — not, however, without giving a look-in at Messrs. Leggatt, and Jennings and Chaplin, in my route thither. I will own, that this " look-in" rather gratified me. I love to see human beings rubbing their hands, and, in the quick movements of their eyes and tongues, giving demonstration that joy was touching their hearts. I found Mr. Leggatt not only in high feather, but in high glee. His prints had met with a prosperous sale. Gentlemen now and then got a little breathing time from that Pandæmonium of speculation (the S. E.) and passing a few minutes with him, frequently scribbled a cheque for a *Wilkie* or a *Turner.* "We shortly expect (said Mr. Leggatt, raising his voice and arms simultaneously) the *Chelsea Pensioners* out;* and then the town will be

* The " Chelsea Pensioners " ARE out—emblazoning numerous shop-windows—delighting the looker-on, and making the purchaser supremely happy. I learn that, already, up-

quite alive." Mr. Jennings received me evidently under the impression that *Annuals** were likely to become *Perennials*. The " Landscape Annual," was to be eminently successful. Mr. Rogers' "*Italy* " had proved a mine of wealth to all the parties concerned. Books, to be sure, were rather on the wane; but Engravings, when

wards of £8000. worth of this print are disposed of—and that the French paper proofs are not yet delivered. Rare doings for Pall Mall !—making the face of the " *Moon* " to shine like that of the sun. 1 remember the painting of this picture : how carefully, how laboriously, how anxiously, the great artist pursued his toil. I see, at this moment, the light-horseman and his charger introduced into the little garden, behind Mr. Wilkie's house in Phillimore Place, Kensington—and, yet more interesting objects, I see the old pensioners flocking round the artist's easel, and marking their several physiognomies—done to the life! It is a glorious production of art: a thoroughly national picture :—but Mr. Wilkie knows that 1 never shall, or can, forgive him, on account of the *Oyster Heresy*. No woman was ever seen opening oysters in June. She might just as well have been selling cherries and currants. I hope yet to have the good fortune to possess an India proof of this interesting composition : but every time that I look at it, I almost heave a sigh that the engraving had not been of such extent as to admit of the faces being a fifth of an inch larger. The Blind Fiddler, by the same engraver (Mr. Burnett,) is to my eye beyond all praise. But . . . what an ORIGINAL !

* I am at war with the ANNUALS; because they are so *very* beautiful, and, like beauties of almost every description, are so likely to be *seductive*. Will they not—may they not —in the long run, be ruinous to the best interests of the GENUINE SCHOOL OF ENGRAVING? Some of the cleverest Artists in the kingdom are engaged in them—engaged, not merely to plough the copper, but in an expectancy of a cer-

embedded in printed text, promised well. A
thousand delicious objects of art were already in
petto. The Heaths, the Findens, and the Pyes—

tain share of profit arising from the sale. This year has seen
the birth of two new adventurers, under the titles of Mr. Heath's
Picturesque Annual, from the designs of Stanfield, and the
Continental Tourist. The former of these is transcendently
beautiful; such silvery skies, and pellucid waters, and delicious architectural accompaniments, have been rarely before
seen. But no subsequent attempt can ever efface from my
memory the extreme gratification I felt on opening the leaves
of the *first* KEEPSAKE. Like " first loves," the impression
is indelible. Much as I admire graphic art, in almost every
way, and regularly as I present my family each year with the
two works mentioned in the text, I must yet throw out the sus-
picion, introduced at the opening of this note,—will not these
Annuals injure the " genuine school of Engraving?" Messrs.
Raimbach, and Burnett, and Pye and Robinson, do not des-
ert that path, which, in due time, will lead them to rival the
" *John Hunter,*" or the *Doctors of the Church,* by the illustrious
Sharpe. On a great scale of Engraving, the Continent beats
us : but the French are absolutely stark mad about our GRA-
PHIC BIJOUTERIE.

Doubtless the " Italy " of Mr. ROGERS (of which the Engravings form by no means its *exclusive* charm) was enough,
at first sight, to take the judgment captive, and to waft the
spectator, in imagination, to the several spots delineated.
Never were text and embellishments so successfully—so happily
—dovetailed. The book rose rapidly in estimation and price :
and it is now at £1. 11s. 6d. a cheap volume. But if the magical pencil of Turner, in these condensed and minute efforts,
appear marvellous, look at the grand Engravings—the one by
Wallis, the other by Pye—from the pencil of the same Artist !
The latter almost makes me forget Woollet. THIS is the
School of Engraving—the style of Art—in which I hope yet to
live to see a *cento* of competitors.

B

the Watts, the Doos, and the Cosins—had more
work on hand than the life of a centenarian could
accomplish : and folks might croak at the West-
end of the town, but with the prospect of Sir
John Key's second mayoralty before them, the
City was never in a more healthy and flourishing
condition." This was the substance of what I
gathered from that most seductive of City repositories of graphic art, of which Mr. Jennings
brandishes the baton of chief command.

I next entered the *Row;* and calling in at
the well-known No. 39, mounted, according to
custom, to the upper regions, where the " Jani-
tor aulæ " received me in his usually kind and
subdued manner. Mr. Reader was not, however,
as I remembered him in "the olden time." Block-
books formed no longer his moveable body-
guard. Editiones Principes, Spanish Chronicles,
and Portuguese Romanceros, had ceased to become his shifting companions. Every thing
venerable and curious seemed to stick with glue-
like tenacity. But to compensate, there were
" brisk doings " below stairs. A whole army of
Lilliputians, headed by Dr. Lardner, was making
glorious progress in the Republic of Literature.
Science,History, and *Art,* each and all contributed
to render such progress instrumental to the best
interests of the body politic—nor, as it became
the credit of such a bibliopolistic fraternity, as
that of Messrs. Longman, Rees, Orme, Brown,

and Green, (there are no more, I believe) was *Religion* absent: for when I descended, I found your " SUNDAY LIBRARY " as a flank company to the " CABINET CYCLOPÆDIA." Will you forgive me, if, in running over the pages of this useful little *Corpus Theologicum*, I remark, that you seem to have stepped out of your ordinary habits, and to have turned a " deaf ear " to the theological " charmers " of the *seventeenth* century? I suppose, however, you have good reason for this deviation from your hitherto established custom.*

---

* It is but right to add, that the Editor of the Sunday Library defends himself, were any defence needful, against any censurable charge on this head ;—by the following remarks in the preface to the sixth and last volume of the work.

" Another consideration, of no secondary importance, has
" also had its weight with the Editor. While he has felt a
" conviction that the sermons of Barrow, South, Tillotson,
" Atterbury, Seed, Sherlock, Jortin, and many others, are
" already before the public in numerous forms—and moreover,
" that the spirit and style of the greater part of these Sermons
" may be said not to be in exact conformity with the tastes of
" the majority of hearers of the present day—(for it should
" seem that there is a *fashion* in Pulpit Divinity, as in every
" thing else)—while the Editor has been influenced (justly or
" not) by a reflection of this nature—he has been also in-
" fluenced by one, which he deems to be of a higher cast of
" character. He has been urged to make this selection, as the
" Reader has it before his eyes, from a conviction, that *modern*
" *days* are not exempt from the display of GREAT TALENTS
" in almost every department of clerical labour; and that, if
" our present Sermons are less learned, less elaborate, less
" divided and subdivided into various branches of enquiry,

I continued my route westerly. Could I pass the Publisher of *Walton* and *Walpole, De Foe* and *Hogarth**—without looking in to see how

" they are eminently distinguished for strength, compactness,
" and perspicuity of style, with earnestness and even eloquence
" of persuasion. There is also, generally speaking, more
" unction—more spiritual consolation—in the majority of them.

" If, on the one hand, there be nothing in the range of
" modern divinity, as it respects Sermons, comparable with
" the magnificent imagery and prodigal copiousness of Jeremy
" Taylor, or with the acute reasoning and energetic diction of
" Barrow, or with the solid learning and masculine vigour of
" Sherlock; so, on the other hand, may we challenge the
" ' olden school' to produce compositions more sweet, more
" winning and instructive, than those of HORNE and POR-
" TEUS; or more luminous and convincing than those of
" HORSLEY and PALEY. And if a spirit of meekness, and
" of almost apostolic primitiveness of character, added to deep
" learning and harmonious style, be sought for, who, in times
" gone by, shall we place above the late gentle and lamented
" HEBER? It were bad taste, perhaps, to eulogise the *living;*
" but the Editor is much deceived, if, in the pages of this
" ' Selection,' there be not found specimens of sound scrip-
" tural analysis, accurate reasoning, and powerful declama-
" tion, which yield to no productions of a similar nature that
" have preceded them." p. vii.

* *Walton's Angler* and *Lives,*—as they are technically called, and as they are put forth by Mr. Major—will continue to
find, as they have already found, thousands of purchasers.
They are the cheapest, prettiest, and completest editions extant. The neatness of the printing, and propriety of the ornaments, are in perfect harmony. When these attractive
volumes (and especially the *Angler*) first appeared, there were
some indirect and clumsy attempts at impugning the HUMANITY
of that most gentle of all earthly creatures, ISAAC WALTON!
—and this, forsooth, because he had given minute instructions

matters, in the way of trade, were going on? I could not: and learnt, with no small gratifica-

about fixing the *frog* and *worm*-baits ! Our publisher's indignation vented itself on the occasion in the following manly sentiments, and vigorous couplets:

> " Go hypocrite ! indulge thy secret hate,
> Of all that's open, manly, good, or great ;
> For slight obliquities affect remorse,
> But act enormities as things of course :
> Spare the *blunt insect* from thy just controul,
> And save thy tortures for the *human soul !*
> Strike at *man's heart*, and then serenely sleep,
> Assur'd the wound is exquisite as deep !"

The *Lives of the Painters*, by Walpole, with Notes by the Rev. Mr. Dallaway, form five perfectly resplendent volumes. The coarse, hard, metallic effect of the heads in the old editions is here transmuted into a natural tone of flesh. Several portraits are engraved from original pictures for the first time: and the new matter, supplied by the tasteful Editor, can leave no doubt of the gradual disappearance of the earlier impressions. In the good old times of Bibliomania, this work would have walked, of its own accord, into the mahogany book-cases of half the Collectors in London.

The *Robinson Crusoe*, with cuts from the master-hand of Cruikshank, to which are prefixed some thoroughly beautiful stanzas by Bernard Barton, contains the purest text of the author extant—from a collation of the edition of 1719, with the subsequent ones. This publication forms two prettily paired duodecimos :—sparkling with wood-cuts. How diversified—how powerful—the talents of the Artist by whom they are adorned ! Look at the cut of Robinson Crusoe (vol I. p. 135,) clasping his hands in extasy, as he throws his eyes to heaven over the treasures first disclosed to his mind in the BIBLE—opened before him ! Then look at his man Friday (vol. II. p. 45,) capering on the discovery of his Father among some captured Indians ! Was ever such wild joy before so delineated ?

tion, that the wheel of fortune had not turned round so capriciously, as, from the general pressure abroad, might have been expected. The *Robinson Crusoe* was " looking up " in the market ; and now that the moralising *Hogarth* was perfected, the Publisher was on the eve of bargaining for a good set of morocco skins, to consign numerous copies to their appropriate clothings.

I then made a slight deviation into Chancery-lane—for the purpose of enquiring how the *Aldine Poets* were going on?—how soon the lordly edition of *Walton**** was likely to blaze abroad in the open day?— and whether the old regiment of *body-guards* still kept their stations upon the shelves? It gratified me to receive rather a comforting answer to these quæres; and when I observed that the large paper copies of your *Bib-*

The Hogarth *Moralised* is, to my fancy, among the most winning graphic volumes of the day. The text is that of Dr. Trussler; but instructive notes are frequently added. the prints are not mere re-engravings from the wretched exhibitions of art in Dr. Trussler's book, but are of a larger form, and executed by some of our best artists. I remember when Dr. Trussler's book once brought the sum of £11. 11s.: so much were the public enamoured of the name of Hogarth! and loved this epitome, wofully as it was executed, of his larger prints. Trussler's old edition now struggles hard, as many a one who has purchased it may, to find a *guinea*.

* The *Angler* of Walton is here alluded to. It is an edition blazing with the choicest graphic art, and likely to become permanently stationary amidst the more costly volumes of a well-furnished library. M. R.

liomania, Tour, Decameron and *Classics,* had not
yet met with a bargainer of mettle sufficient to re-
move them from their present position, I own that
I was well pleased to hear their present possessor
declare, that nothing short of "a good round sum"
should tempt him to part with them—should they
even linger there till doomsday ! Mr. Pickering
had however disposed of his Caxton's *Golden Le-
gend;* which had been carted away as one of the
huge stones to help to build the book-pyramid of
Euphormio.* " But the Jenson and Froben-
loving days (said Mr. P. with a sub-tremulous
note) are gone—never to return ! Who, in these
times, looks at *old* vellums or *young* vellums?†"

Sympathising sincerely in these ejaculations, I
took my departure for the newly established
Repository of Mr. Henry Bohn—who, to his

* If Euphormio *finish* the Pyramid which he is erecting,
as scientifically, and with as good materials, as he has laid
the *foundation*, N** Hall will be the *second* Book-Lion
in Northamptonshire. It is needless to say which is the first.
M. R.

† Of the modern publications lately put forth by Mr. Pickering, *two* have been printed in a very beautiful and highly
creditable manner upon vellum : one, the Holbein cuts, in
one volume, being illustrations of the Old Testament—of which
there were six copies: the other, the reprint of Tyrwhitt's
Chaucer, in 5 volumes 12mo. of which there were only two.
The former were published at £10. 10s.; the latter at £52. 10s.
the copy—elegantly bound in morocco. They are tomes,
which, in the genuine times of book-orthodoxy, would have
caused the eye to sparkle and the heart to rejoice.

credit be it spoken, a long time allowed his *vellum Sforziada* to divide his affections with his newly espoused Bride. Mr. Bohn was as downcast as some of his neighbours; attributing the paralisis in books to the agitation of the question of *Reform in Parliament*—and adding, most justly, that "NOW—or NEVER—was the moment to make extensive and judicious purchases. Considering his short career, as a trader on his *own* bottom, he was thankful for the support which he had received, and was perhaps as well off as those about him—but it could not be denied that there was, at times, sore sighing from the bottom of the heart."

From Mr. Bohn's it was little more than a hop, step, and a jump, to Mr. Thorpe's. I found that redoubted Bibliopolist recumbent upon his sofa—embedded in his books—nothing daunted at the penury of present, compared with former, prices —still concocting catalogues, with a zeal and celerity quite unparallelled*—anxious for their distribution—a Manuscript here, a *Giunta* there —Aldines, the Gryphii—broadside ballads,† and

---

* A collection of all these catalogues would be a curious one; were it only to mark the progressive depreciation of prices frequently attached to the same article: but the possession of all the articles *themselves* would be a more curious result—and infinitely more gratifying to their *vendor!*

† It was late one evening when I caught a glance, and *but* a glance, of a collection of BALLAD-BROADSIDES, very

dainty devices—a "groat's worth of wit," with the " Seven Sorrowful Sobs of a Sinner "— Grolier, Maioli, and De Thou copies:—a grove of sapling duodecimos—a forest of towering folios! Our discourse turned chiefly upon the late sales, and particularly upon that of the *Waverly MSS.* —of which I have before " poured my plaint in your ear." " Would that I had purchased them *all!*" exclaimed the animated Bibliopolist. "Yes Sir, *all.* They would have quitted my shelves within a week of the purchase." But in *other* matters:—tell me, do the " dear Fifteeners " wag their tails, as if about to take a prosperous flight? " Alas, Sir, (replied my informant) they seem, on the contrary, to be tied down by the stiffest birdlime that ever was manufactured. There stand my early Jeroms, and Austins, and Lac-- tantiuses. There slumber my Jenson and Spira Latin Classics. No nimble-footed, liberal-hearted * * * as of old, to visit my retired boudoir, and to tempt me with a "fell swoop!" Everything lingers: everything stands stock-still. The dust on yonder set of Acta Sanctorum will soon produce me a good crop of carrots—from the seed sown there about two-years ago. Lite-

recently obtained by Mr. Thorpe—in a condition, perfectly surprising, and with cuts, occasionally the most grotesque which can be imagined. At the sale of the Roxburghe Library, such a handful of oddities would have brought a great-coat pocket full of guineas. M. R.

rature is perishing. The country is undone." Here the post entered with a letter from a great Etonian Collector, to know if the *Vellum Aldus* had arrived? Mr. Thorpe's eyes sparkled—for an instant only. There was no chance of its arrival. And if it *did*, ought it not to go to Spencer House, or to Cleveland Square?

" Le bon tems viendra" — quoth I to my worthy informant—and some three-hundred steps brought me to Mr. Ackermann's. I found that ever-green Veteran with a mind as active as heretofore. His forthcoming " *Forget-me-not* "*— the parent of that numerous offspring of Annuals, which seem very much disposed to run riot, and to rebel against that parent—was just then preparing to put on its gilded wings to fly abroad; together with its younger sister, the " *Juvenile Forget-me-not*." Mr. Ackermann's Prints, his Pictures, his *matériel* for Drawing and Painting, his publications of fashion and taste, were displayed, on all sides, as radiant as the banners in St. George's Chapel. His activity of mind—his

---

* The *real* parent of the Annuals is the *Buchandler* of the Germans : a duodecimo, printed not very beautifully, upon paper of a second-rate quality. The engravings are the chief attractions. "Upon this hint," Mr. Ackermann "spake "—in his " Forget-me-not :" a pleasing and instructive manual, thickly studded with plates, and of which a good lusty impression of about 16,000 copies is regularly struck off. " The Juvenile Forget-me-not," a comparatively recent publication, may be called a younger brother of its precursor.

courtesy of demeanour—his thorough *germane* bon-hommie—were as conspicuous and pleasant as ever. Still "things were horribly flat. No money was stirring. The young ladies had slackened in enthusiasm. The roses and lilies and lilacs were shedding their lustre and perfumes in vain. Parents drew in their purse-strings tighter than ever. The Reform had frightened away everything. The foreign market was glutted to the very throat."

I then dropt down a few paces to Mr. Cochrane, whom I found as zealously as ever attached to his old Divinity: especially to large paper, or singularly clean, copies of the seventeenth century. The beautiful old morocco folios of Jeremy Taylor and Isaac Barrow, and Chillingworth and Mede, had but recently—after tarrying some nineteen-months—taken their departures. The *Acta Sanctorum* had been courted in vain. Thirteen beneficed clergymen were in the habit of eying it askance—of first taking up one volume, and then another. But no wooer's ardour had yet mounted to the courage of directly " popping the question." The Reform was the real or pretended excuse for holding back. Retracing my steps, I steadily paced onward to the *Castor and Pollux* of Pall Mall:—and there entering a suite of book-rooms, in which, in former times, I was wont to see assembled some of the more eminent *Literati* of the day—Archbishops, Bishops, Earls,

Doctors in Divinity and in Physic, Academics,
renowned in either University—Senators, Judges,
Lawyers, Wits, Poets, and Punsters—I gave
myself up to profound reverie.   Not a mouse
was stirring—in other words, the managing Partner was alone, pacing the quarter deck. . . .

> And started back, he knew not why . . .
> E'en at the sound himself had made!

The master-spirit had departed to a better world.
In imagination, I embodied him, seated in his
arm-chair—his favourite *Sessæ* cat purring by his
side : one leg duly balanced across the other: a
pinch of snuff in his right-hand : his spectacles,
now raised to his forehead—now resting tranquilly upon their wonted seat.   The gentle sa-
lute ... the kind enquiry ... the desultory,
cosy gossip .. the retreat to the brill and beef-
steak*—the Boraccio-flavoured sherry, the full-
bodied port, the fragrant Souchong, the departure " au révoir !" Then again, as touching
" stock in trade." Vellums, large papers, un-
cuts:—Jenson reposing here, Mentelin slumber-
ing soundly there. Azzoguidi and Aldus—Giunti
and Giolito,—Wykyn de Worde and Wyer ..
all intertwined in somnolent embrace. Long sets
and short sets—great Councils and little Councils—Decretals and Dictionaries—Chronicles and
Cancioneros, and poetry without end !

* See *Bibliographical Decameron*, vol. III, p. 152-437.—M.R.

All these things, as I remembered them in former times, came across me in my late autumnal visit ; and I had almost " dropped some natural tears," had not Mr. Foss, seeing my distress, placed before me their last importation from the Continent. MSS. of the Greek Gospels, and Latin Bibles of the twelfth century:—large paper Alduses—vellum Plantins—crackling Elzevirs. The folio Robinson's Hesiod, uncut—the Homeric Eustathius of 1542, in similar condition—and the first Odyssey of 1488, upon vellum!*

But where are your expected purchasers, gentlemen? " Alas, Sir, with the exception of the Eustathius,† all these lovely tomes are likely to become *stickers.* Modern books and ancient books—the *Row* and the *Via Appia*—are equally destitute of attraction. The Reform, Sir, the Reform—or perhaps booksellers, like the Romans, have had their day. Whenever we see cases of old books arrive from Milan, or from Paris, we

* This truly beautiful book was bought at the sale of the library of the late Mr. Dent, for £142.: but alas! it wants its " better half." TOGETHER, bad as are the times—and epidemic as may be the *Cholera*—they would bring hard upon the half of a thousand-pound.

† This Eustathius—with a first Homer, of first-rate quality too—is now the property, as I have been given to understand, of the Rev. E. C. Hawtrey of Eton College. In the Storer Collection, in the same college, there is a copy of this Eustathius, of which the first volume is of a dazzling whiteness—scarcely to be exceeded by that of the snow on Himalaya's loftiest peak !

absolutely lack the courage to open them. Not so in former times. The chisel and the hammer then went merrily to work—and ere you could say "Jack Robinson," the lovely book treasures, membranaceous or otherwise, were arranged in inviting order upon the floor. Within forty-eight hours, up started a tribe of contending purchasers—and the articles seemed to march off in double quick time, as if set in motion by the tap of the drum. How long will it be ere we hear the sound of that tapping again?" "My good friend, (rejoined I—gradually receding towards the small intermediate room, and there becoming stationary), you must be well acquainted with the character of public taste in this country. The moon is not more changeful than that taste is fickle. Things cannot long remain at this very low water-mark—there will soon be an *ebbing*, to be succeeded by a *full flowing tide* of patronage and brisk trade. Let but the Reform Bill pass—and only let MARCUS break the shell of his minority—and you shall see what a broadside of golden balls will be poured into the ranks of yonder closely wedged octavos and duodecimos—all sparkling in their red coats, furnished from the manufactories of *Descuil* and *De Rome*. Take courage. A reaction MUST take place."

I essayed to comfort my friend, but found him with difficulty to be consoled: and with a spirit of dejection, which had now gradually increased since I had quitted the corner of Cornhill, paid my eleventh, and last, visit to the renowned Publisher of the Quarterly Review. I have long considered Mr. Murray as the greatest " FAMILY " man in Europe ; and was therefore not surprised to find him surrounded by an extensive circle of *little ones*. A family man is usually a cheerful man: but the note of despondency was to be heard even *here*. " The Quarterly " was, however, in full plumage—winging its way, and still commanding the attention of an unabated crowd of admirers. Lord Byron was also to come forth in a new dress—shorter, and less flowing—but well-fitting, brilliant, and attractive. So far, so good : yet the taste for literature was ebbing. Men wished to get for *five*, what they knew they could not formerly obtain for *fifteen*, shillings. The love of quartos was well nigh extinct, in spite of the efforts of a neighbouring forty-eight horse power engine, to restore that form to its usual fashion and importance. It was all in vain. There was no resisting the tide of fashion, or the force of custom:—call it as you might. Clear it was to *him*, that the dwarf had vanquished the giant—and that Laputa was lording it over Brobdignag.

Such were the sententious remarks of this discerning and high-spirited Bibliopolist.* On quit-

* Mr. Murray, like the best of us, may have his *capriccios* ; but I KNOW him to possess as warm a heart, and as munifi-

ting his premises, I observed palpable proofs of the absence of those "goodly quartos," which, in former times, the public used to anticipate with such eager curiosity—and which, as containing a BODY OF TRAVELS, were the ornament—and will long continue to be the ornament—of every well-furnished Library.

Sir, I am among those old-fashioned fellows who love a *quarto* "to the heart's core." Gentlemen look more like gentlemen, when such tomes are spread out in rich magnificence before them. The whole is more in keeping. There is greater breadth in the picture : and if a folio or two—historical or topographical—Mr. Sharp's *William of Malmsbury*, or Mr. *Baker's History of Northamptonshire*—be seen as accessories in such a studio, I think this may be considered as the *summum bonum* of bibliomaniacal felicity. There is neither symptom nor apprehension of BIBLIOPHOBIA ... here.

---

cent a spirit, as ever actuated mortal man. He was among the very first booksellers of his day who treated authors, of character and connection, with the respect due to gentlemen. Soft words and civil speeches are *one* thing—and generally mean little or *no*-thing ; but a prompt and spirited remuneration—not the result of minute ledger-like calculations—is *another* thing : and such a thing as Mr. Murray has, in an hundred instances, manifested. As this testimony comes from one who has *not* received *author's remuneration* from Mr. Murray, it may possibly be worth that " renowned " Bibliopole's acceptance.

Before I returned home, I thought I would just step in and see what was going on amongst the *foreign* Booksellers. Accordingly I paid a hasty visit to Messrs. Treuttell, Wurtz, and Richter, Messrs. Bossange and Lowel, and Mr. Dulau. Here I learnt that, at Paris, booksellers were tumbling down like nine-pins. The presses of Didot, Crapelet, and Renouard were all paralysed. Scarcely a tympan or a frisket was flying. Mr. Richter groaned in spirit, when I asked him "how HUMBOLT was going on?" "No, Sir, we are all now for the *fugitives*—pasquinades, revolutionary *rockets* and *squibs*. Not a solid folio stirring. Even Bouquet's immortal work seems to be sputtering in the socket. And *here*—Reform and Cholera make misers put an extra lock upon their iron chests, and keep even adventurous spirits within doors. I have lived twenty-years in England, and never saw the like of these days." I felt half heart-broken as I descended Mr. Richter's flight of steps.

After such a bibliopolistic pilgrimage as that which I have described, I returned to my hotel with a heavy step, and in mournful spirits. I ought however, in common justice, to add, that the book picture here delineated—and perhaps a little surcharged with gloom—may be said to have a somewhat counteracting effect if I notice what usually takes place on *Almanack and Magazine* days. Mere accident put me into possession of a fact, which may be worthy of your notice. Meeting a leading partner of one of the great houses in the Row, as he was threading his way towards Stationers' Hall, I was induced by him to come and witness the dispersion of the *Almanacks* for the ensuing year—it happening to be the last Monday in the month. As we approached the Hall, I saw a crowd of merry scramblers, some hatted, some paper-capped, and more without either hat or cap, pressing the large outer folding doors of the Hall—and joyously clamourous for admission. My guide obtained me an entrance by means of a private door, and mounting one of the tables of the Hall, I saw piles and pyramids of these Almanacks—ticketted according to their respective owners—and to be carried away by the many applicants without. The clock of the Hall struck three; the folding doors gradually expanded—and in rushed the importunate claimants! running in all directions—zig-zag, straight forward, and oblique—pouncing upon the bundles of their respective masters. All was laughter and good humour. Within three minutes, I saw an eight-feet cubical pile of these annual lucubrations—belonging to the house of Messrs. Longman & Co.—disposed of, and taken home; and was informed, by one of the partners, that, before St. Paul's clock would strike eight, every country bookseller's order would be despatched to him by the coach! On further en-

quiries, I learnt that in this article alone, *one*
house (I think it was that of Messrs. Simpkin and
Marshall) paid £4500. for the amount of its traf-
fic. It was also, I learnt, within this same house
that the *monthly publications* were chiefly collected for dispersion—when a scene of equal bus-
tle and good humour might be witnessed.

But I return to my narrative; and with it to
the *hotel* of which I have made mention above.
That hotel (Cooper's, in Bouverie Street, Fleet
Street) was wont to be the place of resort for
Oxford men, for a series of years. It is delight-
fully central; and well calculated for the gratification of most of those pursuits, for the sake of
which, English gentlemen leave their comfort-
able homes, and fancy that, without a *Spring in
London*, their characters stand in jeopardy of being "called over the coals." For a book-loving
man, this street has, from the force of early reminiscences, a peculiar charm for me. At its corner,
old Benjamin White, the Thomas Payne of the
East, once lived, and caused all his noble folios
and quartos to be displayed in skilful and meet
array to attract the curious eye. But why do I
dwell upon *Cooper's Hotel?* Simply to tell you
that, on the very day of my return from my
melancholy book-pilgrimage, I had invited an
old Oxford friend—domiciled in one of the narrow
streets of a City-living—to give me the meeting
over a brace of trout and a roast fowl, and

to discourse as long and lustily as he pleased
upon the topic of BIBLIOMANIA, as it respected
Book Collectors. How the Roxburghe Club went
on? How libraries had been disposed of, or purchased? Who continued " true to their guns?"
And what havoc had been lately made in the
ranks of the more eminent Bibliomaniacs, by that
resistless and " insatiate archer," DEATH?*

I collected from my friend the following de-
tails. " To *begin*," says he, " with the *end*—of
all things. Death hath swept away LEONTES,
BAROCCIO, SEMPRONIUS, ARCHIMEDES, MELIADUS,
and PALERMO.† They were six brave book-
warriors in their day; men who, at sundry sales
which need not now be named, used to

> Flame in the front, or thunder in the rear!

They are now at rest —their libraries all dispersed—their symposia at an end!" Perceiving

---

* " Insatiate Archer! would not ONE suffice?"—YOUNG.

† Under these names were designated the late James Bindley,
Esq., John Dent, Esq., Roger Wilbraham, Esq., John Rennie,
Esq., Robert Lang, Esq., and John North, Esq. Their libraries
were all sold by auction; the first and the last being by much
the most costly in the produce. Of the illustrious engineer,
Mr. Rennie, I possess, by the favour of his son, an impression
of a mezzotint (private) plate, of the portrait of his father,
from the never-erring chisel of Chantrey. There is also a private lithographic print of Mr. Lang, exceedingly like; and
Mr. Douce possesses a drawing of the late Mr. Wilbraham—a
small-whole length—done to the very life. " Ver Ipsissimus."

my friend's voice to be getting tremulous, and
something like a tear to be gathering in either eye,
I bade him fill his glass again—which he did, re-
questing their memories to be drank "in solemn
silence." " But for the LIVING "—resumed I—
"and to begin with ATTICUS."

"Atticus" (replied he) " having exhausted the
libraries of his own country, is gone to rifle the
sweets of many of those abroad. Already have the
Netherlands, France, and Bavaria, furnished him
with the means of making mighty acquisitions.
Already are houses and tenements in Brussels,
Paris, and Nuremberg, crammed with these
treasures :—and what further conquests of this
kind he meditates achieving, it were perhaps vain
to enquire. HORTENSIUS, now elevated to the
Bench, still deigns to look with complacency
upon his 'parchment-kivered' old quarto poetry;
and the Library of LICIUS is yet as full of *witchery*
as ever : but both these Collectors, eminent in their
way, appear to me to be a little influenced by
the *Bibliophobia*—for they seldom or never even
send commissions for purchases. To be sure, the
love of *numismatic* lore hath of late had a strong
influence over the mind of the Baron—producing
a sort of divided attachment between books and
coins: . . and long may he indulge BOTH . . to
any extent or excess he pleases ! I think that
his correct taste and fine feeling will, in due time,
lead him to sacrifice a little of his love of *British*

Coins and Medals for a few acquisitions of *Greek* and *Carthaginian* workmanship. When I say this, I do not wish him to part with his Perkin Warbeck's Groat, HenryVII.'s Shilling, Edward III.'s gold quarter Florin, Henry VIII.'s George Noble, or Edward VI.'s Double Sovereign—all in such very precious condition—to say nothing of the Mary's Royal, Charles I.'s Oxford Pound Piece, and the Medallion of George I. on being made Elector of Hanover. These he may keep, and welcome: and Simon's Petitioning Crown-piece* into the bargain. But a few specimens of the purer Greek, and the winning Syracusan, may not be ill bestowed: although he must despair of a *Mithridates*, and if he even step over into Egypt, will explore in vain for a *Ptolemy Philopater*.†

---

* It has been my peculiarly fortunate lot, to hold in *each* hand one of these "Petitioning Crowns"—concerning which a long gossipping story is extant. Simon was about to be intrigued out of his place in the Mint; and to shew Charles II. to what a state of perfection his numismatic talent had attained, and how little he feared a rival on the score of skill, he struck this medal—"petitioning," round the rim of it, for the retention of his place. To my eye, the device (the head of Charles) wants breadth and boldness, and the hair has a wiry minuteness. The reverse is, I think, very tame and unmeaning.

† Perhaps the *rarest* gold ancient coin in existence. There are *two* Ptolemies—but *that*, with the adjunct of "*Philopater*," is, I believe, only in England : in two collections. France has long languished for it—and the late Mr. Payne Knight almost died for it. The British Museum has it not. The

"Wearied in his pursuit after *Ever-greens*, and·
deeming his quiver of old poetry to be as complete as he can reasonably expect it to be, LICIUS
" rests upon his oars " . . the more so, as he finds
the vessel of life gently dropping down to the
lee shore—where all similar vessels must, in
due course, be locked up in the inner harbour.
Years, my friend, (exclaimed my guest in a
more animated tone of voice, and with considerable expression of excitement)—upwards of
twenty-years have passed away—since the author of the *Bibliomania* described the heroes of
his first auction-fight: and more than a good
round dozen of these twenty, since the *Decameron*
of the same author contained his account of the
second auction contest. Great changes must
occur within such a period. Men not only cannot live for ever, but must be prepared for alterations in their habits, as well as in their looks.
Catalogues are not opened with the wonted activity of earlier life; and the countenance betrays
marks of picturesque indentation. But this case
is not peculiar to Licius—who bears his life's cam-

Ptolemy, *without* the adjunct, is also of such rarity, that it was
not lately in the Museum; although Mr. Young, the coin dea-
ler—the gentle, the urbane, the well-instructed and upright Mr.
Young—shewed me a specimen, which he valued at fourscore
pounds. 1 have handled the *Philopater* Ptolemy—in the
same collection from which I was supplied (for a moment,
only!) with the two Petitioning Crowns—mentioned in the
preceding note : and *what* a collection THAT is!

paign bravely; considering what an over anxious, buffetting, and even agitated life *that* is. There is BERNARDO—turned his Sexagenarian corner— who now lets hawks and buzzards fly unheeded over his head . . all, forsooth, because a copy of his beloved Juliana Berners was knocked down at the freezing price of thirty-five shillings! The report was, that he fainted*—and was carried out speechless from Mr. Sotheby's well garnished auction-room—that this fainting was succeeded by a good, solid, roaring fit of the gout, which kept him six-months within doors—during the whole of which period, the only benefit or comfort he derived, was, from mixing nine-grains of *Ritson's tartar* with three table-spoons-full of *Brathwait's emollient!* The BIBLIOPHOBIA has seized *him*, too—for he scarcely ever budges abroad into a bookseller's shop, and has lately betrayed a very whimsical taste in buying oil paintings, of piscatory subjects, to illustrate his *Waltonian Chamber.* I do not however accuse either of these book-champions of *not* being 'true to their guns.'

* There is another version of this story. It was said, that a bookseller had marked his editorial labours upon this curious old work at thirty-five shillings, in his catalogue—labours, which in better times, used to bring the sum of £12. 12s.! Bernardo took this as a direct insult—and a CHALLENGE was sent forthwith: the field of battle, Little Britain! On a very careful enquiry, I find no truth in this report—although I am not disposed to question the accuracy of the anecdote recorded in the text.

" What a change in HONORIO!—who has now turned his Septuagenarian corner. His glorious library has vanished like the morning dew:—his pictures, finding the separation insupportable, resolved to share the fate of their beloved companions—and *they* too are dispersed, never to be reunited. Meanwhile, their late master resorts again to his *Floral* recreations—to his beds of dahlia and banks of rododendron. He rises betimes to sniff the crisp air of the morning, to hear the lark warble in mid-sky . . .

> The cock's shrill clarion, and the echoing horn !

He is yet firm of foot, ardent in imagination, joyous in discourse . . and, to his eternal praise it must be added, still keeps a delicious specimen of his once beloved *Jenson*, to cheer his heart and delight his eyes. This is a redeeming trait of character which cannot be too much commended. But his LIBRARY was indeed, in many respects, of a most commanding cast of character. To think of Cardinal Ximenes' *own* vellum copy of his *Complutensian Polyglot* being now buried in the vicinity of the Melton Mowbray hunting Club! His Vellum Didot Horace—unique in ALL respects— and lately clad in the exquisite garniture of Charles Lewis*—is *well* placed in its present si-

---

* Charles Lewis lavished the whole mystery of his art upon this capacious and exquisitely got up folio. See it noticed in

tuation. Euphormio makes it a sort of book-shrine, of which he most religiously keeps the key. But if I look back at the sale of any *one* article, out of this extraordinary collection, with more satisfaction than another, it is in the acquisition of the Luther Bible* by the British Museum."

Finding my friend's voice here beginning to grow a little rough and wiry, I begged he would replenish his glass—and proposed " the health of *Honorio*—as honest a whig as ever quaffed *Rudersheimer* in the genuine green-embossed glass"— by way of a sweetner to the draught. He drank it with enthusiasm, and continued. "PAMPHILUS, the nephew of Honorio, is unflinchingly true to his guns. He throws out his lead, to sound carefully as he goes—but when he gets into water shal-

the *Decameron*, vol. III. p. 139. It cost Mr. Hibbert £140. in boards—in which state it was purchased by Messrs. Payne and Foss, at Mr. Hibbert's sale, and sold, as above mentioned, to Euphormio. Charles Lewis, latterly, had *open* days for company to come and gaze upon it. The unrivalled Willement depicted the coat of arms of the present owner, on the vellum fly-leaf, and drew the patterns for the silver-gilt clasps. I should pronounce THIS to be the most tasteful, as well as most gorgeously bound, volume in Christendom ! M. R.

* This had been the property of Mr. Edwards, and is fully described in the *Decameron*, vol. III. pp. 123-4. It was purchased at Mr. Edwards' sale for £89., and was sold at Mr. Hibbert's sale for £260. I saw it carried triumphantly into a hackney-coach; and within twenty-minutes of its departure, it was deposited in the British Museum. M. R.

lower than " quarter less five," he puts the helm
about, and makes directly for port. I can scarcely
mention so *virtuously seductive* a book as his illustrated copy of Mr. *Ormerod's Cheshire* I have
known a large party kept in perfect good humour,
full twenty-seven minutes after the dinner had
been expected to be announced, by turning over
its leaves, emblazoned with heraldic embellishments by the skilful and indefatigable Thomson
—and I think you will allow this to be a pretty
severe test ; as no crisis of human existence puts
men's patience so sharply upon the tenter-hooks,
as *that* which precedes a *dinner*—when the party
is all arrived. You may try a *Chronicle* printed
by *Verard,* or *Gratian's Decretals* by *Eggesteyn,*
but it is dull work: it won't do: the ladies throw
a freezing glance; the elderly gentlemen yawn.
No, my friend, it is at *such* a crisis that we want
embellished volumes—missals, radiant with burnished gold—or topography, illustrated like the
Ormerod's Cheshire of Pamphilus. Still, I understand that nothing hath been stirring of late
in the library of Pamphilus—no additional weight
to try the strength of his shelves: neither folios,
nor quartos, nor octavos. All remains *in statu quo:*
and content to rest on his oars, as a successful
Editor of Mysteries, and archœlogical expositor
of Elizabethan Carriages, he shrinks from the task
of any farther developement of British Antiquities. It should seem as if the fear of *Reform,* or
of *Cholera,* had been at work here.

" Philelphus has lately accomplished a singularly bold achievement. Unwilling or unable
to throw out his net to entice more fish, he has
chosen to trim and adorn, and make much of,
those that remain in his custody. Of your friend
Dr. Dibdin's Decameron, he possesses a copy
bound in ten volumes, ornamented to suffocation
with embellishments. Charles Lewis had a *carte
blanche* to do the needful in *his* way; and such a
series, or congeries, of graphic illustrations—
comprising everything remote or capricious—
was surely never before concentrated or brought
together. A party might be kept in good humour from dinner to supper-time by a studious
examination of its contents. But it is time to
make mention of Crassus and Prospero. The
former is still wedded to his Topography and
English History—and has lately made himself
master of a copy of *Picart's Religious Ceremonies*,
for which no cost was spared to render it an acquisition of the very first water. There are few *spreads*
equal to that of the spread of *these* volumes. I
know of no parallelogram-shaped library which
has a more joyous, yet chaster aspect, than that of
Crassus;—and although he, like his friend Pamphilus, rarely ventures into deep water, still it is
pleasing to see how gaily he trims his wherry,
and always contrives to keep the wind setting ' in
the shoulder of his sail.'*

* " ——— lenis crepitans vocat Auster in altum."
Aen. lib. iii. 70.

" It will delight you, I am sure, to hear that
PROSPERO is yet in the full exercise of his ' en-
chanter's wand '—yet ' true to his guns '—which
he sometimes double shots and treble shots. His
maple-wooded bookcases rejoice the eye by the
peculiar harmony of their tint,—with the rich
furniture which they enclose. Here a bit of old
bright stained glass—exhibiting the true long-
lost *ruby tint:*—there, an inkstand, adorned in
high cameo-relief, by the skill of John of Bo-
logna:—a little regiment, pyramidally piled, of
the rarest China cups, out of which seven successive Emperors of China quaffed the essence of
bohea. Persian boxes—Raffaell-ware—diptychs
and chess-men—the latter used by Charles V.
and Francis I., on their dining together, tête-a-
tête, not long after the battle of Pavia. Korans,
Missals, precious Manuscripts, Marc Antonios,
Albert Durers, Roman Coins—the very staff with
which Regiomontanus used to walk on his house-
top by moonlight, after making certain calculations in his calendar!! Magic lore, and choice
Madrigals sung by Queen Elizabeth's private
band: brave prick-songs!—and the parchment roll
which Handel wielded in beating time on the first
representation of his Messiah. But his belles-
lettres — facetiæ—old poetry—and rare prints,
form a combination which hath no compeer!—
and, Septuagenarian as he is, I wish him a good
score of years yet to shot his guns, and to fire
them off with effect.

" PALMERIN, whose hermitage is described in such glowing language in a certain work, is yet enamoured of his *Romaunt Lore*—though he has bade a long adieu to his rural residence at Stanmore. London and Ryde now alternately receive him. His gothic taste yet finds a snug corner to develope itself: his drawings, paintings, old-furniture: cabinets, replete with curiosities—armour—nodding plumes, breastplates, halberts and quarterstaves—two-handed swords—billets and battleaxes! It were idle to attempt a *catalogue raisonné* of such a picturesque mélange—but his BOOKS still preserve their wonted ascendency:—and long may they continue so to do! MENALCAS must not be forgotten:—though his books cease to maintain their original position. A truer Roxburgher never toasted Christopher Valdarfer. Heavy were the groans that announced the resolution—arising from high and honourable motives—of parting at once, and for ever, with the treasures which were contained within his celebrated parallelogram-shaped library.* Certes there was no fear of Reform or of Cholera operating here. Ah, my friend, manuscripts and

* Over the door, on entering, of this long-cherished bookretreat, was the following inscription—in capital letters.

" Ervta Pontificvm rabsis penetralibvs olim
　　Mirère antiqvas vellera passa manvs
Aetatis decvmae spectes indvstria qvintae
　　Qvam pvlcra archetypos instrvat arte dvces
ALDINAS aedis iniens et limina JVNTAE
　　Qvosqve svos STEPHANVS vellet habere Lares.

printed volumes alike put on wings and fly away!
Books as well as sovereigns become *locomotive.*
Your decanter, however, is *stationary.*"

This reproof was perhaps merited; as my attention had been wholly absorbed by my friend's
narrative. Replenishing his glass, I requested
him to give me a brief outline of the *status in quo*
of the ROXBURGHE CLUB, since the last notice of
it in your Decameron. "Willingly;" replied he.
"To begin with the venerable and illustrious President. I rejoice to learn that he presided with
his wonted vigour and effect at the last meeting.
A few gaps, made by that resistless trespasser,
death, have been filled up since the publication
just alluded to;* but the literary labours of the
Club proceed languidly. *Havelok* was the last
performance of any note; and I am not singular in
the expression of my regret that the *plan* adopted
which led to *that* publication† has not been rigidly

---

* The more recent grafts upon the old stock have been as
follows:—The Earl of Cawdor, Viscount Clive, the Hon. and
Rev. Neville Grenville, Sir Walter Scott, Bart., John Arthur
Lloyd, Esq., Archdeacon Wrangham, and the Rev. Charles
Edward Hawtrey—" good men and true "—in ALL their
bibliomaniacal bearings!

† That Publication was edited by FREDERICK MADDEN,
Esq. of the British Museum—at the united expense of the
Club; which, at the moderate charge of £6. 6s. the copy, obtained possession of probably the most intrinsically curious
book it had ever put forth. Nor is Havelok of meagre di-
mensions. His form is portly, and his garb is attractive.
The preface and the glossary are equally creditable to the

followed up in subsequent efforts. The BANNA-
TYNE CLUB seem, in this respect, to be very much
shooting ahead of the parent-Society.* The

talents of the Editor. Report says, the same able hands are
now employed upon a very interesting old English metrical
romance, called The WER WOLF, written by an Earl of
Hereford, from an unique MS. of the fourteenth century, in the
library of King's College, Cambridge:—as the first votive
offering to the Club from the EARL OF CAWDOR. A fund
of entertainment is expected from its perusal. Havelok had
one fate attendant on its publication. It provoked a little
etymological controversy between the Librarian of the Royal
Institution and its Editor: men, both of too amiable a temper
to take delight in literary fisty-cuffs. Mr. Madden stoutly
replied to the attacks of his Critic. As stout a rejoinder was
threatened—but never appeared. Of late, however, both
Assailant and Defender were seen cordially shaking hands
across the same MS. in the British Museum. Si sic omnia!
M. R.

* The publications of the BANNATYNE CLUB, which are
more numerous than those of the Roxburghe, confirm an opinion
which I have long entertained from earliest manhood—namely,
that the narrative of an eye-witness of events is worth all the
up and down, and rambling, and frequently contradictory, conclusions of the most ingenious historian upon record. One
simple *fact* is worth one hundred *conjectures;* for, in the absence of *fact*, what mad pranks are sometimes committed by
the most sober historians! Inventories, also, of goods and
chattels—be the same wearing apparel, jewellery, or *books*—
are infinitely amusing, and sometimes instructive. But the
Bannatyne Library has other pretensions to notice and commendation: essays, disquisitions, reports, records, and other
such materials, form a rich store of information deserving alike
the attention of the antiquary and historian. CATO PARVUS.

While upon this topic, my friend might have noticed the
Household Books of Expenses of Henry VIII. and *Queen Mary*

symposium of the Roxburghers now takes place on the second Thursday in May, owing to the lateness of the season when the anniversary of the first sale of the Boccaccio happened.* At this symposium, there is less protracted revelry than heretofore. The 'albescens capillus' has a mighty effect in making men keep orderly hours. No dawn-of-day retirement, as in times past, for ** and *** The toasts are now confined to Christopher Valdarfer and William Caxton: to which add, 'THE CAUSE OF BIBLIOMANIA ALL OVER THE WORLD.' When *that* sentiment ceases to be given from the chair, good-bye to the Club! The triumph of BIBLIOPHOBIA will *then* be complete."

Here my friend raised his voice to an unwonted pitch, and vehemently struck the table as he pronounced the last sentence. It might have been in consequence of the last *replenisher*—but he proceeded, collectedly, to say, "there is yet good hope that the gallant breed of Roxburghers is not likely to be speedily extinct. Vigorous shoots are springing up, and making way, promising to become sturdy branches as the old timber falls to

---

—as edited by Sir Nicholas Harris Nicholas and Mr. Madden. They are very curious volumes, and based upon that of the famous *Northumberland Household Book*, of which the well-known Bishop of Dromore was the Editor. These latter volumes are also published in singularly good taste, as respects beauty of exterior. M. R.

* On the 17th of June, A.D. 1812.

decay. Why will not ULPIAN hold himself in readiness to start at the first opening? He is eminently entitled to present himself as a candidate. His collection of books is at once choice, costly, and copious; and no man loves to embed himself more thoroughly amongst them . . . His pillow case, *Columbus's Letter* of 1493, stitched to the original *Challenge* of *Crichton*: his counterpane, all the *large paper Hearnes*, formerly in Dr. Mead's library, still glittering in their primitive morocco attire: his mattrass, *large paper Dugdales*: his bed curtains, slips of the original *Bayeux tapestry!* When he takes to *Illustration* of any particular work, he takes to it in right earnest, and with a glorious, yet appropriate, prodigality of embellishment. I conclude that he prefers his *Lettou* and *Machlinia Littleton* to every other book in his library—with the exception of his *Jenson's Bible.* To his credit also be it spoken, he is a great encourager of *booksellers;* and is not emulous of entering the lists of bidders, when he can secure an article at a quiet price in Chancery Lane, or in the vicinity of Covent Garden. No fear of Reform or of Cholera ever depresses his hopes, or slackens his progress in the genuine straight-onward course of the BIBLIOMANIA. Russia leather is, with him, the charm and protection against epidemic miasmata of every description; and give him but the treble-rowed entrenchment of his library, he snaps his fingers alike " at the arrow of fate and the canker of care." Moons wane or enlarge without his notice, so long as a *Piranesi* is to be perfected, or a *De Bry** to be rendered complete.

* Report has pronounced the copy of DE BRY, in posses-sion of the above gentleman, to be the fruit of incessant toil, for a series of years—at an expense, little short of hundreds upon hundreds. It is said to contain the first editions of the Grands et Petits Voyages, as well in Latin as in German, throughout—also, the second editions in Latin, and the Me-rian edition — with the *original* and *reprinted* Elenchus— the English edition of the Virginia (the first part of the Grands Voyages)—the Abridgments of the Grands Voyages, three editions, 1617, 1631, 1655—and three volumes in quarto, in German, published by the family of De Bry, and the work of Las Casas, edition 1598 :—also, nearly a complete set of all the first and original editions of the voyages from which the De Bry formed their collection. To these are added a complete set of the Collection published by Hulsius in Ger-many, twenty-six parts, second editions—and a fine set of the *first* edition of that Collection, except parts 11, 12, 13, 14, 15, 16, 17, 24, 25, and 26. The third edition of the Abridg-ment of the Grands Voyages, 1655, contains, besides the fourteen parts, two additional voyages, which are not in De Bry, but are included in the Hulsian Collection. It also contains every variation and peculiarity mentioned by De Bure, Camus, or De La Serna, except in the Grands Voyages, Latin—part 2, one leaf, containing on it, Frankfort, 1591— part 4, the twenty-four plates, *without* the numbers engraved on them—part 5, the frontispieces to the Text and Plates, *without* the word " Hiä " interlined — part 6, frontispiece to plates, with pasted table ; in the centre, " Sequuntur Icones," &c.—part 10, frontispiece, Vessels Sinking, not a Naval Combat. M. R.

I will not presume to undervalue the copy of De Bry thus summarily described ; as, living remote from the Metropolis,

"And why may not DECIUS aspire, in due time, to a similar honour of becoming candidate on a vacancy among the Roxburghers? Far off be the day which may occasion that vacancy—but, as come it *will,* let Decius then mount his courser, all covered with membranaceous housings, and spring into the arena—a champion to win the fight! He hath pretensions of no common kind. He loves books, and he knows all their bearings, within and without. The dappled calf, and the red sprinkled edges of one compartment of his library, are duly relieved by the morocco tint and diamond gilt tooling of the other. He revels in bindings of Padaloup, De Rome, Roger Payne, Montagu, and Baumgarten. His French folios of archæological lore and graphic embellishment, stand proudly pre-eminent;—and for Greek and Latin Classics, who, for an unbeneficed Divine, shall step in before Decius? To my fancy and peculiar taste, how-

I stand no chance of ever seeing or handling it. But the pages of the *Library Companion,* (pp. 372-6, *Breeches Edit.* see p. 8, note ante) furnish me with such a description of a copy of the same work, in the possession of the Rt. Hon. Thos. Grenville, as seems to set all competition (and peradventure none may be intended) at defiance. If I were inclined to *break in* a young book-collector, by giving him rough and hard exercise to perform, I would set him upon the completion of what may be called the *ordinarily perfect* copy of the Peregrinations of Messrs. De Bry:—but, even here, I must bargain for the *true Elenchus.* CATO PARVUS.

ever, his *Manuals of Ethics and of Divinity*, in the
seventeenth and eighteenth centuries, exhibit
specimens of a rare and happy coincidence in the
pursuit of the Bibliomania. Let Decius, I say,
be ready to start at the first sound of the trum-
pet which gives notice of a vacancy to be filled
in the Roxburghe Camp."

Here, my friend ceased from his narrative ;
which, as it had occupied a considerable time,
and had embraced a variety of topics extremely
gratifying to my feelings, called forth my heartiest commendations. " One glass more," —
quoth he—" and we part. I drink to the health,
happiness, and longevity of the ILLUSTRIOUS
PRESIDENT of the Club of which I have been
discoursing:—the founder, as well as the possessor, of the finest private library in Europe. God
bless him !" So saying, he dispatched a copious
libation of sparkling sherry, and sprang forward
to seize his walking staff—to make good his
retreat homewards—but, as if something of importance had suddenly come across his recollection, he turned round upon me, and enquired,
" whether I purposed quitting London on the
following day." " Assuredly so "—replied I.
" Be it so then "—resumed he—" but promise
me faithfully, ere you start, that you will step
across the water and take a peep at the new
Library of Lambeth Palace." I pledged myself faithfully so to do—when my friend hurried

away, under the impression of being too late
to attend a vestry meeting, which had been especially summoned for that evening. On the
following morning—which happened to present
itself with the least possible portion of a London
fog, or mist—I made haste to carry my friend's
parting request into execution ; and taking boat
at the Temple Stairs—the tide serving—I glided
quickly under the two bridges of Waterloo and
Westminster, (of which the first will long continue to be the world's wonder!) and was duly
put on shore opposite Lambeth Palace.

As, however, I had never seen it under its
new aspect, I was for a little time lost in reverie
on its approach : so much so, that the boatman
asked, "whether I wished to go on to Vauxhall
Stairs?" There was indeed good cause for such
abstraction or reverie. I could scarcely credit
the evidence of my own eyes....

Miraturque novas frondes, et non sua poma !

exclaimed I, as I caught the first full glance of
the entire range of the building. But the Library—is alone our business now. You, Sir,
may have probably seen it again and again—and
I think I may challenge at once your admiration
and thorough approval of its plan. What a
goodly garniture of antiquated tomes ! How
harmoniously all the architectural accessories

blend with the precious treasures which they enclose! We have all the characteristics of a genuine University library—transplanted on the banks of the Thames! " And can this be (said I to myself) the old *Juxonian* hall,* through which the winds used but lately to whistle, and of which the pavement was dank, and the light doubtfully transmitted? It is even so." My guide seemed to enjoy my moody raptures exceedingly; adding—(probably on the supposition, from the trim of my dress, and fashion of my hat, that I was a thorough rustic gentleman) that " my admiration might perhaps be easily accounted for, when I was informed that Mr. BLORE was the architect of the whole concern." " I heartily wish"—rejoined I—" that all concerns of this kind were managed in the same sensible and satisfactory manner. I am delighted —yea, more than ordinarily delighted—at the happy transformation before me. I could gladly linger in such a book-domain through the four successive seasons of the year, and gather fruit

* This Hall was built by BISHOP JUXON. Its principal exterior beauty is, the boldness of the buttresses; but there appears to be, near it, a beauty of no ordinary loveliness in my antiquarian eyes. I mean, a vane or weathercock—broad, bold, with elaborate, open work, yet light and picturesque. I long to see it regilded—and the whole surface of the Lollard towers, and of the side facing the Thames, restored—as I know *how* it is capable of being restored—by the correct master-hand of the architect above mentioned.

at every quarter." Here, I thought my guide seemed to eye me as if I were a gentleman subject to occasional aberrations of reason, and pressing me towards the door, seemed to desire my egress. I thanked him very heartily for his civility, and, much as I wished to become acquainted with other portions of the building, was obliged, from the pressure of time, to make towards the water's edge, and to seek my boatman — who was in attendance, expecting my return. As I resumed my seat, I could not help casting frequent glances upon the glorious pile I had just left behind—and which confirmed me in the truth of what I had often heard of its present Most Reverend Occupier; namely, that he had exhibited the talismanic art of a certain Roman Emperor, in leaving behind him "*marble*," that, which, on his first possession of it, he found to be only "*brick*."

Urging my boatman to make his best exertions, I returned in time to my hotel—to prepare for a mid-day departure from London: not however without a previous call upon my opposite neighbour, Mr. Abraham John Valpy;—before I got into the Windsor Coach to make a little détour through that place, Reading, and Oxford, in my return to Laurel Lodge: resolving to see, in those several towns, whether the *Bibliomania* or the *Bibliophobia* prevailed. Mr. Valpy was in any mood but that of *in alt.* His *Thesaurus* had run its course—nobly, but not productively. The scoffs, gibes, and jeers which it had endured in its progress, were now forgotten: the rubbish was swept away—the scaffolding removed—and the building, a PYRAMID in size and durability, stood out complete. As the work of one editor, and as the labour of one Printing Office, it might challenge, as it would be sure to receive, the applause of posterity. " But the *Delphins*—tell me truly—how do *they* go on?" Mr. Valpy was silent. He need not have been so. If the work had expanded immensely, it was not from an exclusive wish to enrich himself, but to render it the more serviceable to students in classical lore. There was an elaborate collation of the earlier editions—an "ordo"—notes, grammatical and illustrative—a critical commentary—copious indexes, together with a carefully corrected text—all deserving of the most decided commendation. But fashion had had its sway here as in other matters. At starting, it was the fashion to subscribe—at the present day, it was the fashion to strive to throw up the subscription: yet the work had gone on as zealously and honestly as ever. After all, it was the best *octavo set* of LATIN CLASSICS extant; and a day would come —not improbably in that of its publisher—when its general merits would be acknowledged by an increased price, as well as by the warm eulogies of the learned. To have planned such a work, and to have carried that plan into such extensive effect, placed the Publisher in the very foremost rank of his class.

With observations like these I strove to cheer my old acquaintance; advising him to take courage to his heart, on the completion of the Herculean task which he had undertaken. His elementary publications were " going on swimmingly;" and many other works, on hand and in prospect, seemed to augur well. " He had braved the tempests of the years 1825-6, when his Brethren were wrecked by dozens; but such a DEAD PALSY in the bookselling line, as that in the *present* year, he never could have brought himself to believe. The very *sight* of a book—especially of a *subscribed* book— threw some men into a delirium of horror. It was "Φέυγε μαλ,"* with Homer—or "avaunt, quit my sight!" with Shakspeare.† Oh, Sir! (added he, in a tone of no ordinary feeling) let the Reform Bill only pass—let the vessel of state only once get well trimmed, and it will go gallantly over the waves! Men will return to their *lares*, and to their ordinary pursuits—speculative or active. There will be chasms to fill with books, which had never been before discerned : walls to cover with pictures, which had never before come under contemplation. Commerce will then put on her

---

* Iliad, *lib.* i, 173.
† Macbeth.

hundred wings, and fly to every quarter of the globe."

Being unwilling to damp the ardour of my friend's imagination, and by no means disposed to dispute the premises upon which his conclusions were drawn, I wished him a good day—observing, as the deliberate conviction of my understanding, in accordance with the best wishes of my heart, that " I felt persuaded a very palpable RE-ACTION would take place in the course of the year 1832." Within the four ensuing hours, I found myself walking upon Windsor Terrace. The day was fine. The breeze was soft. The landscape, as all the world knows, luxuriantly picturesque. My object, however, was BOOKS—or rather *Literature* and *the Book-Trade.* After a turn or two in that fairy land of a sunk garden, at the eastern extremity of the Castle, I retraced my steps, and, catching a peep of the " antique spires," (so sweetly celebrated by Gray) pushed on towards Eton College. There, was the *Storer Collection*—and there PRISCIAN was domiciled : Priscian, the classical and the accomplished. Books are his " dear delight "—and Bibles, among those books, the primary objects of attraction. He shewed me a rare set of them—such as, in a private collection, are eclipsed only by those at Kensington and Althorp. There were also belles-lettres —in abundance—in the German, Spanish, and

Italian, as well as in the French and English, languages. But oh, that splendid *MS. of Ovid!*—approached with delicacy, unlocked with care, and surveyed with extasy!—"Δὸς δ'οφθαλμοίσιν ἰδέσθαι"*—exclaimed I, as, on turning my eyes in an opposite direction, I essayed to see the numerous folios and quartos—some of which were impervious to the glorious sun-beam.

Having lost my list of memoranda, taken on the spot, I grieve to say that my account of this classical retreat must be thus superficial. But it is only the performance of an act of common justice to add, that the Falernian and Mark Brenner of Priscian crowned the evening's hospitality of his abode. I quitted such a residence with reluctance; especially as I had so many inducements, unconnected with my passion for books, to make a longer stay. But my time was limited. To say nothing about the laurels, growing wild and unseemly about the "Lodge"—and standing in daily need of their master's pruning-hook—(for I allow no one to trim them but myself) I had, in fact, undertaken the execution of a somewhat arduous task in accomplishing the journey in contemplation.

By eight in the morning I was stirring—visiting, before my final departure, the book-shop, which, under the mastership of *Pote*, once boasted

* Homer's Iliad, *lib.*xvii. 646.

of no contemptible reputation. Here, in the heart of the town—and at mere arm's-length, as it were, from the college—I expected to have found an early *Lilly, Holt, Stanbridge,* or *Whittinton.** But no such good fortune attended me. Even the editio princeps of the Eton Grammar, as now in general use, was not to be laid hold of. Abruptly retreating, I made towards the high road, and found myself in due course upon the top of a Reading stage. On reaching that town— the abode of my earliest boyhood—I hurried down London Street, into the Market Place, and Minster Street, to pay an immediate visit to Messrs. Rusher & Son, and Mr. Smart—the renowned booksellers of the place. The latter I had known from my twelfth year: and twenty years ago we had done a stroke of business together—when books were *run after,* and a brisk and liberal circulation of cash afforded the means of *catching* them. Mr. Smart sighed heavily as our hands were conjoined. " You come, Sir, (said he) at a sad, sad time—when my books are hanging down their heads, and there is nobody to pat and to cheer them. Mount my great Repository, backward. What will, or can, you see

---

* An account of the works of these illustrious men—the great LUMINARIES OF GRAMMAR in the earlier half of the sixteenth century—will be found in the second and third volumes of the *Typographical Antiquities of Great Britain:* Edit. 1810, &c.

worthy of a moment's notice—much less of carrying away as a trophy? Customers are alive only to Reform-discussions. There is a knot of them, assembled here of a market day, which does not disperse till nearly dark. They turn their backs upon my books: and my *History of Reading*, of which your old friend and first schoolmaster, John Man, was the author, is allowed to remain *in statu quo* upon my choicest library shelf." I expressed great sorrow at this intelligence, but the only comfort I could impart, was, that he partook of "neighbours' fare."

Mr. Rusher and his Son received me right cordially: but here, again, all was dark and disheartening. Their love of books was as great as ever: their enthusiasm, unabated: but their customers—those best feeders and supporters of "love" and "enthusiasm"—were gradually falling off:—and as for *Bibliography* (with the exception of the staunch Collector on Forbury Hill), there was not a creature that cared a pin's point for Dr. D.'s multifarious labours in that department. "Look you, Sir"—added Mr. Rusher, jun.—" we have tracts out of number, appertaining to the period of the two Charles'—but who vouchsafes to open them? Who reads them? Who regards them? Who bears them away? And then for *Topography*, and the *Gentleman's Magazine*—you may as well ex-

63

pect to catch a sturgeon in the Kennett,* as to secure a customer in these formerly highly favoured departments of book-collecting....

> " I sigh and lament me in vain ;
>   These walls do but echo my moan:
> Alas, it increases my pain
>   When I think of THE DAYS THAT ARE GONE!"

At this instant—and producing a sort of magical effect—in walked the " staunch Collector " just alluded to — the classical and bibliographical NESTOR of the borough town of Reading. A cordial salutation followed the first expression of surprise ; and we had almost entered upon a discussion of the relative merits and demerits of Schedules A and B, when young Mr. Rusher observed, that, " as the day was getting on fast, we might possibly like to take a little refreshment in his father's back parlour ?" This, however, was courteously, but firmly objected to by Nestor ; who insisted upon my accom-

---

* Pope, in his Windsor Forest, has recorded the renown of this river for its " silver eels." It runs, in a bright and rapid course, nearly through the centre of the Town—and receives, I believe, several tributary streamlets in its way. In early youth—when summer suns were warm, and summer skies were clear—1 have often doffed my garments with my school companions, to plunge into its "translucent wave." Of these companions, TWO only survive, to my knowledge! M. R.

panying him home, to his boudoir of belles lettres—whence the Thames was seen, winding its
beauteously picturesque course—margined by
meadows, upon which hundreds of cattle were
grazing—the lordly domain of Marsack (once
that of Cadogan,) crowning the neighbouring
mountain-height . . .

A happy rural seat, of various view !

I instantly obeyed the Octogenarian's sum-
mons; and a few hundred yards brought me
within *that* library, which, in the happy days of
Bibliomania—some fifteen years ago—I had entered with greater glee of heart than at present.
Wherefore was it so ? The books were the same.
The bindings were the same. The former had
not grown either taller or shorter : the latter
had obtained still greater beauty of tone, by the
course of time—in an atmosphere, not reachable
by a London fog. But my dejection continued
—in spite of the urbane upbraidings of " mine
host." " What care I "—quoth HE—" for the
capriciousness of public taste ? Shall my first
folio Aldine Demosthenes and Rhetores be less
coveted—less embraced—than heretofore ?

Dear as the ruddy drops that warm my heart,

shall be, to me, my Elzevir and Olivet Ciceros !
Nor let old Scapula and Facciolati droop their

towering heads—and, shew me the man, who shall dare to undervalue my large paper Barnes' Euripides, West's Pindar, and Potter's Lycophron ? Will any creature, short of a confirmed idiot, presume to " write me down an ass," because I have over and over again tossed up my head at the pitiful offer of three-score and ten sovereigns for my large paper *Grenville Homer ?* Perish all these dear delights !—perish their owner with them !—sooner than he shall lend a helping hand to the dissemination of that hydra-disease—BIBLIOPHOBIA ! Welcome typhus—welcome scarletina—welcome even CHOLERA ! Pitch your tents, and mark out your victims as ye please. Number ME among them, if it be your good pleasure—but let me die . . . hugging my HOMER !

My friend here became momentarily breathless. His action had been " suited to the word :"—and he sunk exhausted upon the soft wadding of a chintz arm-chair. I hurra'd him as he fell! On recovering, he smiled placidly, asking me if " I thought he had been *wandering ?*" " Wandering!"—replied I, quickly—"quite the reverse ; you never spake more to the purpose: never more directly to the point. All your remarks went strong and straight forward . . . like the arrow to the bull's eye of the target. Give me your hand—and with it possess my heart! While such sentiments as these possess an *Octogenarian,*

E

shall I listen to the puling plaints of a cow-hearted dabbler in book-purchases? Shall I endure a lengthened, and perhaps torturing, negotiation about beating down the prices of Vellum Spiras and closely cropt Caxtons? Can I suffer the Alduses, the Giuntas, and the Frobens, with our dearly beloved Wynkyn De Worde, Pynson, and Julian Notary, to be shoved quietly ' to the wall,' and make no effort to rescue them from such ignominy of treatment? Never: while I have the power to wield an arm or plant a foot. I take a lesson from your gallantry of spirit —and am well-nigh ashamed at my querulous sympathy among the Metropolitan bibliopoles. Your sweet air and bright skies make me feel and see as I ought to feel and see—' I am a man again!' ''

Forgive, Reverend Sir, the dramatic air of this part of my narrative; but the whole incident has been so vividly impressed upon my recollection, that I know not how to dispossess myself of it—and I give it you with a most literal veracity. In essaying to take leave, I found there was no escaping a Nestorian *Symposium*. My friend having scribbled hasty notes of invitation to the Rectors of the three parish churches, to partake of this symposium, we then strolled abroad—and were drawn insensibly towards the ruins of the ABBEY. Just at that time, there was a great ferment in the town—whether these ruins should be preserved, or not, by subscription, from their meditated destruction by the owner of the property on which they stood:—and this subject formed one of pretty brisk and incessant discussion during our dinner. The Vicar of St. Mary became frequently *poetical* (no very unusual thing with *him*) in his deprecation of such a meditated act of vandalism. " Certes," said I, " it is the principal and proud feature of your town; and it is moreover the palpable link which connects you with the twelfth century. Give me the russet tint of the flint stones of which these ruins are composed—the ragged and picturesque forms into which time and accident have now cast them—and I care not a rush for all the flaunting brick and bath-stone structures of which the town and its neighbourhood may boast." There was, in fact, not one dissentient voice among the guests. Even BOOKS were forgotten—while we dwelt, in imagination, or in discourse, upon the " by gone days," when this magnificent structure was reared.* Now, its

* This abbey was " reared " in the time of Henry I; and is perhaps more than eight centuries standing. Like many of the edifices of those days, the walls of this Abbey seem to have been built for eternity. There are views, out of number, of their picturesque character and position ; but those which represent them before the building of the present gaol upon their site—about forty-five years ago—exhibit them in larger masses; as a great portion was compelled to be destroyed for the building in question. In digging the foundations of this gaol, human skeletons out of number were found—said to have

ruins seem, comparatively, but "the shadow of a shade!" " Tempus edax rerum"—observed our host, in a sort of " *sotto voce* "—bidding us not spare his port of 1811 *(" Vin de Comet")* as an antidote to the melancholy which such a subject was likely to engender.

We broke up at ten. The moon was at full: unobscured by vapour, mist, or cloud. The meadows seemed to be sleeping beneath her soft lustre....

And drowsy tinklings lulled the distant folds!

We made a little circuit, or détour, by the side of those ruins which had elicited such ardour of discussion. We paused before their "grey and battered sides"—now softened by the pale tint of the moon-beam. We became instinctively mute .... listening to the "stilly sound " of every thing above and below! Not even the note of

been buried there in the time of Cromwell, from a battle which took place in the neighbouring meadows. Some of the *existing* fragments are from six to nine feet in width—and defy destruction, except from the force of gunpowder. If the town and corporation of Reading suffer these fragments to be destroyed, from the lack of public spirit, they affix the seal of indelible disgrace upon their corporate character. There is certainly no saying to what extent *individual cupidity* may go—but for the sake of all their past glories, I hope the Inhabitants will make a NOBLE FIGHT for the preservation of these adamantine relics! I feel well persuaded that Mr. H., the senior Alderman, will be " fetlock'd in blood " ere he relinquish the contest!

the inhabitant of the " ivy-mantled tower " was heard. Every-thing seemed . . .

Insensible . . . . as those that slept beneath!

" What a night!—What a spectacle!" Not another word was spoken :—such *Tacitus*-like brevity being infinitely more natural and impressive than the circumlocutory periods or speeches of *Livy.* We parted, therefore, convinced that our eloquence had suffered no diminution by the use of the interjections only just uttered. The next morning, I had some thoughts of taking a run down to Bath and Bristol—to see how Mr. Upham at the former place, and how Mr. Strong at the latter, were carrying on their bibliopolistic speculations. But I wanted courage. In spite of the effort made in my reply to the book-veteran, Nestor, I found that the wailings of Messrs. Snare and Rusher were yet tingling in my ears, and depressing the barometer of my spirits. It is towards OXFORD, therefore (said I to myself) that I will set my face, and direct my instant course—and for that venerable City I secured a place on the roof of an Abingdon and Oxford Coach, which was to depart about three in the afternoon. Purley, Pangbourn, Straitley, and Abingdon, are the villages and towns in the route thither.

Doubtless, Sir, you have, in your Oxford days,

made a similar trip—or at any rate have bowled down the hill, which, 'twixt Abingdon and Oxford, gives you the first full view of the towers and turrets of the venerable ALMA MATER. Thirty-eight years have passed away since I first made this descent—but never, even in the warm glow of youth, did the objects before me appear more splendidly striking. The sun was sinking rapidly —upon what seemed a pillow of molten ruby and amethyst, fringed with burnished gold. Light streaky clouds of alternate pink and opal, canopied his couch. The high arch of heaven " was in a blaze with his descending glory."* The towers of Christ Church, All Saints, St. Mary, All Souls, and the Schools—with the dome of Ratcliffe—were vividly spangled with the general radiance; while portions of the several buildings, below, were embrowned in a dark, soft, warm shade. Towards the extremity, Queen's, and the tower of Magdalen, carried on the line of picturesque beauty and grandeur; and the hill of Shotover, in the distance, was enveloped in a magical hue of purple. The meadows and the elm-roofed walks of Christ Church—the Charwell and Isis commingling into one bright, broad, and gently gliding stream—upon the surface of which, boats and sailing vessels were swiftly darting along, and interchanging positions—

* Burke.

catching the departing sun-beam upon their sides
—ALL THIS, and much more which escapes minuteness of description—presented itself to my
view as I descended the hill in question. Oxford
is perhaps no where seen to greater advantage.*
But, I was not so light of heart—so buoyant in
spirit—as at the period before alluded to. Life
had had its REALITIES. The mind had had its
SHADOWS. There had been sorrow and grief and
disappointment, and .... DEATH! As I reached the
bottom of the hill, and neared the City, me-
thought I heard the *chimes* of the several Colleges
and Churches—when the beautiful lines of Mr.
Bowles's Sonnet " *On Revisiting Oxford*" came
immediately to my recollection.

> I never hear the sound of thy glad bells
>   OXFORD! and chime harmonious, but I say,
>   (Sighing to think how time has worn away)
> Some spirit speaks in the sweet tone that swells,
>   Heard, after years of absence, from the Vale
>   Where *Charwell* winds!"†

But I hasten to more matter-of-fact detail.

---

* The present venerable Dr. Huntingford, Bishop of Hereford, used to say, that "he never came down this hill without
taking off his hat—as a respectful salutation to ALMA MA-
TER." I believe one of the very best views of the University,
by the magical pencil of Turner, is from this spot.

† The remainder may as well be here subjoined : for the
whole is eminently sweet and touching. Indeed, after all, it

Within an hour, I was in Broad Street with Mr. Parker—the Corinthian pillar of Bibliopolism at Oxford. But our meeting was not as of old. The notes of wailing soon got the better of those of congratulation. There stood *Reimar's Dion Cassius, Duker's Thucydides, Hudson's Josephus*—all in the portly forms of large paper, and in the princely garb of red morocco .... but who were likely to be the purchasers? The *Ciceros*, from Leyden, Paris, Geneva, and his own Oxford,* all long standing dishes .... getting cold .... to be looked at, and not tasted! Even the *Clarendon Press* productions, in their peculiarly attractive octavo forms .... all

Fallen from their high estate—

as if paralised by Cholera or the Reform Bill!

may be questioned whether the Rev. W. L. Bowles be not the *facilè princeps* of living Writers of Sonnets? The remainder is as follows:—

> " Most true it speaks the tale
> Of days departed, and its voice recalls
>   Hours of delight and hope in the gay tide
>   Of life, and MANY FRIENDS now scattered wide
> By MANY FATES! Peace be within thy walls!
> I have scarce heart to visit thee; but yet,
>   Denied the joys sought in thy shades—denied
>   Each better hope, since my poor * * * * * * died,
> What I have owed to THEE, my heart can ne'er forget."

C. P.

* That of 1783, 4to. 10 vols. See a tale, connected with this edition, in the *Library Companion*, p. 579, Original Edition; and p. 586, Second Edition.

Advancing towards a comparatively obscure corner—in which, in former days, I used frequently
to stumble upon a crackling Elzevir or an uncut
Aldus—I took up a very handsomely printed
Prospectus of a work of which I had never before received the slightest intimation. Judge,
Sir, of my surprise when I found that YOU were
once meditating a *Literary and Local History of
the University of Oxford.** Mr. Parker begged

* As, in after times,—when the Reform Bill and the Cholera shall have worked their good or evil—and men's passions
shall have pretty generally subsided, by giving way to their
reason,—if such an " after time," in this ever-agitated country, (" cet isle, plus enragé que les mers qui l'environnent,"
observes Montesquieu) shall arrive—a brief mention of this
Secret History in Literature, may be as pleasing to a few others
as to my friend Mr. D'Israeli, in particular. Happening to
possess a copy of the Prospectus in question, I think the
reader may not be disinclined to be put into possession of a
portion of it.

" ALMA MATER OXONIENSIS. A HISTORY
OF THE UNIVERSITY OF OXFORD.

" ADDRESS.—It cannot have failed to strike every lover
of his Country's Antiquities, and every admirer of its Graphic
Art, that there exists NO Publication which can be deemed
worthy, in all respects, of transmitting to posterity, a correct,
as well as an enlarged, account of the Antiquities, architectural and literary, of the UNIVERSITY OF OXFORD. The
" secret indignation " felt by Loggan, nearly a century and
a half ago, may be yet felt, with some slight modification, at
the present day : namely, that, " while rural mansions and
obscure villages have fonnd Chroniclers and Artists, the
University of Oxford remains without any adequate represen-

that I would carry it home with me. "It will at any rate amuse, if not instruct, you"—said

tation of its numerous architectural attractions." This is the spirit, if it be not the literal version, of Loggan's observations.* &c. &c.

" To the lover of Picturesque beauty, it is impossible to behold the many-turretted buildings of the University—the solemnity of its retired cloisters, and the grandeur of its " Academic Groves,"—without a wish that such interesting objects might find an adequate record by the hand of Art:— while, to the meditative understanding, such objects are clothed with additional splendour from the recollection that Oxford has been the " NURSING MOTHER " of Statesmen, of Legislators, of Divines, Philosophers, Poets, Historians, Scholars, and Philologists: of illustrious characters . . . . . .

> " Whose honours with increase of ages grow,
> As streams roll down enlarging as they flow!"
>
> POPE.

" Nor is the interest attached to such a publication likely to be purely local or even national:—for where is the civilised quarter of the GLOBE in which the fame of this distinguished University is not established? To give therefore to posterity, and to the learned of all Countries, AN ADEQUATE IDEA of the variety of interesting objects to be combined in a well executed HISTORY OF THE UNIVERSITY OF OXFORD,—as well as to afford delightful reminiscences to the former Inmates

---

* Loggan's remark is as follows: " Occasionem huic Instituto præbuit tacita quædam indignatio, cùm viderem rustica passim tuguriola, et ignobiles pagos, summorum Artificum cælo et penicillis inclarescere, OXONIUM interim, celiberrimum Musarum domicilium, quo pulchrius aut beatius quidpiam Sol non conspicit, *intactum* præteriri," &c. OXONIA ILLUSTRATA. 1695, Folio *(" Spectatori Ingenuo".)*

he. " What encouragement (replied I) did the planner of the work receive?" " None (re-

of her classic Walls—it is proposed to publish *Three Folio Volumes,* which shall embrace the following departments of art. 1. Picturesque Views of the University, under different aspects. 2. Views of the several Colleges, Halls, and Public Buildings—in whole, or in part—as the subject may require. 3. Interiors of Chapels, Halls, Libraries, &c. 4. Gothic Architecture : Figures : Niches : Screens : Entrances, &c. 5. Modern Sculpture : Figures and Busts of Eminent Men. 6. Portraits of Distinguished Characters, ancient and modern ; including several which have never been before engraved. 7. Curiosities, Relics, &c. 8. Book-Illuminations.

" Engravings of these, and of similar subjects,*—executed from Original Drawings—by Artists of the first celebrity in their respective departments—will, it is presumed, give a distinctive character of excellence to *this Publication* which will be in vain sought for in its precursors. It is intended that each Volume shall contain at least *six* large and elaborate Plates of *Landscape* or *Architecture,* or of a union of both; six *Portraits,* engraved in the first style of excellence : eight Copperplate Vignettes, of a large and finished description—and numerous Wood-cuts. But, in proportion to the desire which every affectionate son of ALMA MATER will feel for the existence of such a splended memorial as is here submitted to his consideration, must be the anxiety that its execution be *certain* when once it be *determined upon ;* that every requisite measure be adopted to protect it from casualties, as well as to distinguish it from the characteristics, of an ordinary undertaking. The plan will be so matured, and the number of *Literary Coadjutors,* engaged in its execntion, will be so well

---

* The fronts of such Colleges, Halls, &c. as have been *rebuilt,* or have undergone material alterations, will be engraved as they appear in their *original* forms, from the views of Loggan, or from those prefixed to the earlier *Oxford Almanacs.*

joined he) but what appears on the face of the
Prospectus ; and of the names there recorded,

acquainted with that plan, that, if set on foot according to the
anticipations of its Author, scarcely any supposable contin-
gency can frustrate its completion. In accordance with a just
anxiety on this important point, each volume, as delivered,
will be considered as complete within itself—in regard both to
the text, and the decorations by which it will be accompanied.

" The name of ANTHONY A-WOOD has been long and
justly popular among the lovers of Oxford Antiquities. The
labours of that Antiquary were doubtless both arduous and
meritorious; and the Public have been recently put into possession of the most valuable portion of them, as connected
with the *Lives** of the more eminent characters of the University. Wood's Collections, or Annals, relating to the different
Colleges and Halls, have also their peculiar advantages; but,
under both points of view, as a Biographer and Topographer,
that author's researches were too miscellaneous; and, at times,
too trifling and unimportant. He chronicled the minute and
the marvellous, with the same assiduity and degree of good
faith as he did the important and the veracious; and a result
has followed which might have been naturally expected:—his
works are a Repository for occasional consultation, in which
however the reader cannot obtain the more valuable matter
of which he is in search, without wading through toilsome
pages, encumbered by puerilities, and defaced by unconquer-
able prejudices. Yet, as a *Substratum* whereon to build
firmly, let no Oxford Antiquary disdain to avail himself of
many of those materials, which, but for Wood's unremitting
perseverance, would have irretrievably perished. Nor must
the name of HEARNE, a zealous disciple, as well as enthusiastic admirer, of Anthony à-Wood, be forgotten among those

---

" The ATHENÆ OXONIENSES: edited by the Rev. Dr. Bliss,
Public Registrar."

not THREE were obtained at Oxford. I believe, Sir, the affair never proceeded beyond this announce. The author, with his usual characteristic zeal, was sanguine to excess. He counted upon a large muster-roll of subscribers—but the day was GONE BY! An angel from heaven could scarcely effect such a work *now*."

I slowly folded up the Prospectus, casting a sorrowful glance at its contents—of which I resolved leisurely to make myself master at my Inn—the *King's Arms*. I will fairly own to you that I was, at first, alarmed at the magnitude of the design; but what will not a union of *hearts* and *hands*—consolidated by a liberal remuneration— effect? The next morning I visited Mr. Talboy's; and we had a good long gossip together. On groping 'midst the volumes in the rear of his

---

Writers who have treated of the Antiquities of Oxford. The incidental notices of the University, scattered throughout the multifarious publications of Hearne, will be carefully investigated, and duly appreciated: and where the information appears to be authentic, it will not fail to be recorded. To say that the notices of Hearne are free from the imputation of credulity, would be to assert what is foreign to the truth."

The price of the work was to have been £7. 17s. 6d. the volume, small paper; the large paper, £12. 12s. the volume. Only thirty-two names were received; of which six were put down for large paper. May more fortunate hands accomplish the execution of such a splendid—and, in more than one sense, NATIONAL—undertaking! To have failed, in such times of literary torpor and fatuity, can be no disgrace to its Author. CATO PARVUS.

shop, I stumbled upon a dingy little tome, entitled "*Elogia Sepulchralia*," &c., of which one P. F.* was the author—and was mightily pleased with the motto in the title-page, which runs thus:

"Miramur periisse Homines? Monumenta fatiscunt."

AUSON.

" Nescia MUSARUM sed MONUMENTA mori."

OVID.

" Englished by a Wit of the Age:

" Men timely die, and Princes day by day
Moulder to dust: but BOOKS WILL LIVE FOR AYE,
And re-embalm us in the coldest day!"

On reading it, I could not but be struck with its application to your projected *History of the University of Oxford*:—and was almost horrified to find a copy of the Prospectus on Mr. Talboy's counter, defaced and rendered scarcely legible by dust and ashes. That energetic Bibliopole sympathised sincerely on its failure: adding, that, although the said Prospectus had been deposited at every common Room, and with every Head of a House—many of them also with the leading Tutors of the University—yet, the impression of his mind was, that only ONE assenting

* " Typis impressit Author P. F. [Payne Fisher] Ex Equestri Familiâ Generosus: necnon tam Collegii, quam Campi, Graduatus. Lond. 1675. 8vo. Impensis Authoris, et in Authoris usum solum Typis exarata." By no means an every-day book. M. R.

voice, in the way of subscription, had been transmitted to its Author." " *Whose* might that be ?"
—observed I. " Dr. Routh's "—replied my
Informant.

At the mention of *that* name, a thousand agree-
able flutterings took possession of my breast. I
learnt, as I am sure *you* will too, with no common
satisfaction, that the intellectual buoyancy of that
eminent scholar was unabated; that years had not
enfeebled the powers of his mind, nor dimmed the
lustre of his eye : and that he was yet as awakened
as ever to all that was precious and instructive in
the lore of the primitive Fathers. A visit, paid to
him—shortly after leaving Mr. Talboy's—confirmed this good account. I found him as cour-
teous and as communicative as ever : correcting, if
I may so speak, a proof sheet of his beloved *Lac-
tantius* with one hand, and the pages of a new edition of his favourite *Burnet* with the other. His
hall, staircase, corridors, dining room and drawing room, contained the same goodly book-furni-
ture as of old—outvying, in intrinsic worth, all the
velvet and silk and chintz hangings of the proud-
est palace in Christendom. Mr. Chantrey was, at
the moment, on a visit in the University ; and a
whisper was current that he was not to leave it
without carrying the head of the President of
Magdalen College in his travelling carriage with
him to London. As this could easily be accomplished without *decapitation* of the Original,

I expressed the heartiest wishes that it might take place. Still I had doubts and fears.

My next personal object of visitation, was my old friend the Public Registrar: whom I rejoiced to find hale, hearty, active—and as obliging as ever. I had known him in the times of the BOOK-FEVER—symptoms of which I *rejoiced* to observe yet hanging about him! His area is small, but it is well filled:—and no man is so little disposed to let apprehension of Cholera or the Reform Bill upset his bibliomaniacal felicity. " But when, my friend, (remarked I) do your *Hearniana* appear? Horace's precept has been doubly observed—for more than *twice nine years* have stolen away since you announced the publication of that interesting work." He replied, that " he could not help himself—his business, as public Registrar, was so unintermitting, and of such essential importance, that he feared he must bid it an eternal adieu." The latter words fell tremulously from his lips—and it was clear to me that, at heart, he was as " sound as a roach " in the *legitimate cause.*

On quitting, I made instinctively for the BODLEIAN LIBRARY: for that dear, old, favourite abode, yet haunted by the spirit of all those great *Book Collectors* who have figured away in the pages of your Bibliomania. The *master-living* Spirit of the Library was, as usual, prompt to receive me, and to receive me cordially. We

walked, and sat, and stood, and walked again—
in that interminable forest of printed books and
MSS. of every description. Dr. Bandinel gave
me a sketch—necessarily a rapid one—of the
acquisitions which had been more recently made;
and, among them, placed before me the stupen-
dously splendid monument of the spirit and liberality of one individual—in the *Mexican Antiquities*—of which Lord Kingsborough was the Pa-
tron. The copy before me was UPON VELLUM—a
present from that Nobleman. It was justly arranged among the Lions, yea of the roaring lions,
of old Bodley: and for my part, I wish the noise of
such roaring may extend to the uttermost parts of
the empire. A similar copy (as I learnt) had been
deposited in the British Museum, also a present
from the same munificent quarter. I confess that
I was transported at this intelligence; and while
such liberal and noble blood was glowing in British veins, I would not despair of the revivifi-
cation and ultimate triumph of the BIBLIOMANIA.

Dr. Bandinel then shewed me a variety of book-
curiosities, of which I could not help wishing that
you had been also a spectator. At five, in company with the Public Registrar, I found myself
at his table—well garnished—and stimulant of
the " feast of reason, and the flow of soul." At
first, we were rather flattish. It could not fail to
be so. I had communicated my conversation with

F

Messrs. Parker and Talboys:—the tenor of which found sympathy in their bosoms: but "the health of my Lord Kingsborough"—("toto corde et totis viribus") made the heart-vessels dilate; and in a trice we were all in an overflowing glow of sentimentality! The hock had a more racy flavour: the peaches, a more juicy distillation. The declining sun had a mellower lustre—and the breeze of the evening wafted a more delicately aromatic fragrance to our senses. We forgot the Cholera—and even the Reform Bill; and resolved never to forego, or even to cause to be mitigated, our attachment to VALDARFER and to CAXTON! Night came on—and, with it, a moon of equal amplitude and splendour with that witnessed at Reading. We strolled in the Gardens of St. John—those gardens, in which Brown declared that the whole strength of his genius had been concentrated. They give indeed " ample space to narrow bounds " with so much happy art, that I know of nothing which must be mentioned in the same breath with them—considering the nature of the *site*, and the limits within which they are formed.

Here I parted with the worthy head Librarian of Bodley, and pursued my course homeward, in company with my friend the Public Registrar. As usual, I went to take a peep at that matchless quadrangle of Public Edifices, of which St.

Mary's and the Schools form the opposite sides, with the Ratcliffe Library in the centre.* I went, as usual, to visit this spot of enchantment by moonlight . . . and found it, if possible, more magnificently impressive than ever! You must be wearied with description, and therefore I shall only say, that, strolling backward and forward with my friend for some half hour, we talked of days gone by, and of days that now were—sincerely believing, in our hearts, that a RE-ACTION, equally bold, decisive, and beneficial, would within a few months take place: that, not only the hearts of Messrs. Parker and Talboys would *there* be made to dance with delight, but the hearts and reins of every deserving Bibliopolist in the empire *also*. My friend was firm in action, and loud in voice, when he made this declaration . . . so much so, that he awakened the echos of the place . . . and I thought that I once heard the re-echo of " Re-action " dying away within the cloister of the Divinity School. The next morning I paid a hurried visit to the " rich and racy tomes " of Caxtonian lore, which are duly locked within the press of the first Library at St. John's; and did not fail to cast an interested, but not longing, eye upon the peculiar, but limited, treasures of the black-letter kind,

* They have lately put an iron railing, of an oval form, round this building—an adaptation, as infelicitous as unnecessary. C. P.

which they possess at Exeter College.* I was
compelled to tear myself away from all these
book-felicities, as the various College-chimes re-
minded me of the hour of setting out for " *Laurel Lodge.*"

In my way hither, it was but natural to muse
upon all that had taken place in the spot just
quitted. I candidly own that it strikes me that a
very great improvement in the education of
young men at Oxford and Cambridge, might be
easily effected. The undergraduate, who first
loves his Pliny or his Propertius from the cut of
its coat—alias the fashion of its binding—may,
in a happy moment, by looking into its text,
love the author for his *own* sake. The young
mind should be directed to new objects. That
perpetual system of *Herodotising*, *Thucydidising*,
and *Euclidising*, is enough to render the sharp-
est intellect obtuse .... in the long run. And
Sanderson and *Watt*— can these *Genii* do anything towards awakening the fancy and refining
the tastes of young men, verging towards their
twentieth year? Consider, with what high expectations, and sometimes high capacities, young
men are sent to College; and how much it
may be in the power of the Tutor to apply these
capacities and expectations to their most obvious

* Why will not the *Magnates* of these two Colleges put their
book-treasures, of *this* description, into secure and appropriate
bindings ? **M. R.**

and honourable uses. Teach young men—especially those who are heirs to large properties,
and to a splendid ancestry — where the noble
feats of their forefathers are recorded in the
pages of the County Historian—and they will
become lovers, and peradventure collectors, in
that branch of the *Literæ Humaniores.* The name
of DUGDALE is equally proud and imperishable.
Should they love *Poetry?* Tell them how Milton altered both thought and word in his first
effusions, and they will buy all the varieties
of the early impressions of that great man's
muse. For Shakspeare, there will be no end to
the *chasse* in the eternally varied field connected
with the earlier editions of his Plays. An acci-
dental visit to Suffolk made the public acquainted
with a Prompter's surreptitious edition of *Hamlet,* a year earlier than any known edition of that
play.*

* The library of Sir Henry Bunbury, Bart. M.P., (at Burton Hall, near Bury St. Edmond's) contained an edition of
Hamlet, of the date of 1603—unknown to all Commentators
and Collectors. It had belonged to Sir Thomas Hanmer, his
maternal grandfather; and was bound up in a volume of
choice rarities in the Dramatic line, and other early editions
of Shakspeare. This volume—light in weight, but ponderous
in value—was disposed of to Messrs. Payne and Foss, in ex-
change for a number of useful publications; and by Messrs.
Payne and Foss was sold to the Duke of Devonshire, the
possessor of the finest dramatic library in Europe. Before
parted with, Mr. Payne caused a literal re-print of the *Hamlet*
to be published, of which 500 copies were struck off. It made
some noise at the time—but the text was evidently not the

But, above all things, when the generality of
young men can wade knee deep into the streams
of Grecian lore, without the fear of catching
cold—in other words, when they can master
Greek and Latin sufficiently well for the ordinary purposes of philological research—imbue
them with a love of ANTIQUITIES: of antiquities,
including the passion for gems, coins, and architecture—and this will lead to the acquisition of
the *best works* relating to such an essential feature
of a library. See also that the study of NATIONAL
antiquities be duly inculcated; so that, in travelling through a country, every hillock of earth,
and every fragment of stone, may be taught to
be viewed with an eye of no ordinary interest.
I hold this to be a species of *Patriotism* in its way.
Anything and everything that recals to us the
past periods of our country—that re-peoples the
temple of the Druid, or the castle of the Baron—
is of immediate and direct use, by teaching us to
weigh, and to estimate accordingly, the *present*
positive blessings which we enjoy. And as we
are careful of the *past*, so may we be attentive to
the *future*. Not a coin, not a gem—not an inscription upon a stone tablet, however time-eaten
—not a frieze, not a capital, not a pedestal, in
the architectural pile—will *then* be contemplated

offspring of Shakspeare's brain. Amongst other oddities, the
Ghost is made to enter in his *night gown and slippers!* See
the *Library Companion*, p. 813, Second Edition.

with indifference : and, with this, a most zealous
attachment to those *Written Records* by which a
true knowledge of history is mainly upheld. Thus
a new *sense,* as well as a fresh *impetus,* is given
to the human understanding; making all the
difference between the vacant gaze of an ordinary traveller, and the intelligent remarks of an
instructed observer. Thus, PHILANDER, once
deeply versed in the tragedies of Aeschylus and
Sophocles, on a sudden dispensed with the ser-
vices of those Dramatists; sought no longer pleasure in choruses, semi or full ; but became smit-
ten only with Pausanias and Dion Cassius—and,
from them, by a natural transition, sought his
chief solace in Montfaucon and Piranesi, Cam-
den and Gough : resolving to devote the remainder of his life (yet wanting many years of its
grand climacteric !) to the study and acquisition
of our *National Antiquities.* And thus, to ad-
duce no other instance, does the Master-Spirit
which yet inhabits and adorns *Stourhead,* pursue,
indomitably, his enthusiastic course ! The snows
of age sit lightly upon his brow; and bodily in-
firmities neither damp his ardour nor enfeeble his
exertions: while

Summer suns roll unperceiv'd away,

as the spear of the Aboriginal Briton, or the
mystic urn of the Druid, find entrance within his
Studio.

Is the Collegiate Pupil destined for the CHURCH? let him not only construe freely the Bible, the Apostolical Fathers, and the Antiquities of Eusebius, Sozomen, and Theodoret, in their original tongues, but let him feel an equal anxiety and pride to possess himself of the best editions of the original text. From the dead, he will naturally come to the living, languages—and among these, his Tutor will, as naturally, tell him to cherish that which is his OWN. What a prospect then awaits him! You anticipate what I am about to say. You anticipate the acquisition of MSS. of *Wiclif's* Version of the Sacred Text*—the *Tyndale*, and *Coverdale* printed Versions—heading

---

* It is a joyful note of intelligence to impart, that, at length, we are about to receive a most carefully collated, and I will add, GENUINE PRINTED TEXT of the MS. version of the *Old Testament*, by Wiclif: the New Testament having been published by Lewis, some fourscore years ago, in folio, and reprinted by the Rev. Mr. Baber, of the British Museum, in 4to. 1810. The Rev. Mr. Forshall and Frederick Madden, Esq. (see p. 47 ante)—both of the British Museum—are also the Editors of this forthcoming *first edition* of the text of the Old Testament; and these are names which justify every reasonable expectation of complete success. The Clarendon Press, to its immortal honour, prints it gratuitously. Of the various MSS. of the original, that copy in the library of the British Museum (formerly belonging to the Royal Society) is perhaps the most intrinsically valuable, as well as splendid : and that, in the library of F. Douce, Esq. is probably the *facilè princeps* of those in *privaie* collections. I think I have seen nearer twenty, than twelve, copies of the original MS. : all about the commencement of the fifteenth century. C. P.

the folio set of *Matthews, Taverner, Cranmer,* and *Parker.** Anon, for our earlier Rituals, Prayer-Books, and Sermons! The race is set before him in all its fascinating varieties; and PORTIUS starts to reach the goal of a never-dying renown. The longest life is too short to gratify his inextinguishable passion: the largest room, in his father's mansion, too small to admit of his marshalled treasures ... in the black-letter department only. He sighs for an hundred feet gallery; in which to arrange his busts of our early Reformers; and his day dreams and his night dreams run riot upon the acquisition of choice copies of LATIMER, CRANMER, and FOX.† The

* It may be as well to refer to the summary, but spirit-stirring, account of these Bibles, to be found in the *Library Companion,* pp. 30-32: and if the reader (such an one as POR-TIUS probably is) chooses, to the other larger authorities there referred to. But of all these early English Bibles, place ME in the front of the copy of *Cranmer's* (1540) UPON VELLUM, which is usually kept in the Lodge of the Master of St. John's College, Cambridge!! " Obstupui, steteruntque comæ, et vox faucibus hæsit!" This has occurred more than once—to *me*—and to more than *one* Roxburgher! Of the first edition of the COVERDALE Version, I believe it is hopeless to think of ever obtaining a *perfect* copy. That, in the library of Castle Ashby, belonging to the Marquis of Northampton, approaches the *nearest* to perfection of any with which I am acquainted. Well may my friends Messrs. John and Arthur Arch, muster up their courage to proffer £100. for an entirely perfect copy ! See p. 15. In a more or less *imperfect* state, I should say few of our earlier Bibles are of such common occurrence. M. R.

† I presume that the *Sermons* of the first, the *Catechism* and

Ecclesiastical Chronicles stand also prominently conspicuous to his mind's eye—and for a perfect Parker, *De Antiquilate Ecclesiæ Brittannicæ*,* he would cut off the entail of nine roods of the best arable land upon the paternal estate! Every stick, every stone, every relic—once belonging to that illustrious Archbishop—is an object approaching almost to adoration with Portius; and should he ever see, as it has been *my* good fortune to see—in the archives of Corpus College, Cambridge—the *sacrament cup*, and the *salt-cellar* (of Milanese workmanship) which once adorned that great man's altar and table, I am not quite sure whether the President of that Society might not require the aid of two lusty University beadles to prevent . . . something like an act of sacrilege ensuing!

Such was the general and perhaps rambling

certain devotional pieces of the second, and the *Martyrology* of the third, are here alluded to. Of these desirable publications to a student in our English Theology, the *first* edition of the last work—in 1563—is the GRAND object of securement. The only thoroughly perfect copy of it, with which I am acquainted, is *that* in the library of the late Philip Hurd, Esq. and to be sold by auction, with the entire collection of his books, under the hammer of Mr. Evans. I hear with pleasure that the Son of the deceased will at least *equal* the book-celebrity of the parent. C. P.

* There is no end to discussions touching the *materia bibliographica* connected with the work here mentioned—first published in 1572, folio. Those copies in the collection of Lord Spencer, Mr. Grenville, Mr. Coke, Mr. Douce—to say nothing

train of ideas which occupied me, on quitting my beloved *Alma Mater*, till I reached this secluded spot. Behold me, then, back again at *Laurel Lodge :* embedded 'midst my books; with no sound but that of the choristers chattering in the grove, and " the low of distant kine "—while the village spire, peeping over the slope of the hill, every now and then affords a sort of comforting exhilaration of spirits. Sir, I will hope that this little Tour has not been made in vain. I will hope that, if I have commenced this epistle in the strain of despondency, I may conclude it in that of comparative exultation. There is doubtless a frightful falling off in the " good old cause," amongst the many: but amongst the " GALLANT FEW "—of which the number is not *very* small—we see spirited resolutions followed up by unabated energy and liberality of conduct. Nor is it a hopeless symptom of the times, that two rival English Versions of *Richard de Bury's Philobiblon* are, I believe, at this moment in the press. If ever a man should revive the spirit of his great Predecessor, De Bury, it is THE PRESENT Lord Chancellor: who, I make no doubt, would do all in his power to go beyond him. In regard to the *Patronage* of *Literature,* what can exceed Lord Kingsborough's patron-

of the Cambridge and Lambeth copies—are the most perfect which I have seen. In fact, it might be doubted whether *two* copies were ever found *alike.* C. P.

age of the *Antiquities of Mexico,** a work put forth
by Augustine Aglio? There is hardly any con-
ceivable case, more likely to challenge and to
obtain the applause of posterity, than *that* to
which I allude. We have here a gallantry of
spirit which puts all precedent at an incalculable
distance behind. It may be thought indelicate to
mention more *names;* but I may make allusions
to *persons.* The libraries of St. James's Place
and Althorp, can hardly receive ANY acquisition.
If not full to overflowing, they lack nothing
essential. The honourable and high-minded
owner of the library in Cleveland Square, suffers
not one jot of attachment to abate towards his
books—and it is but the expression of mere common justice to say, that SUCH books merit all the
intensity of devotion by which they have been

* This magnificent performance consists of seven large folio
volumes, of which the first four are plates, and the remaining
three text. The author, or editor, is AUGUSTINE AGLIO.
Lord Kingsborough is reported to have devoted £25,000. to
its execution, in the successful manner in which we now view
it, and in which posterity will not fail to appreciate it. Such
Lordly munificence is so rare, so splendid, so deserving of
perpetual praise, that I know not how to express myself as I
feel upon the subject . . .

> In freta dum fluvii current, dum montibus umbræ
> Lustrabunt convexa, polum dum sidera pascet,
> Semper honos nomenque tuum landesque manebunt
> Quæ mecunque vocant terræ . . .
>
> Virg. Æn. *lib.* i. v. 607.

See p. 81. ante. C. P.

acquired. Years neither damp the ardour, nor slacken the exertions, of their owner; whose judgment is yet as ripe, and whose taste yet as refined, as ever. On its *scale*—and of its class— (and the scale is far from being a stinted one) it puts all competition at defiance. I observe, however, that you have said pretty nearly the same thing, in your last edition of the *Introduction to the Classics.**

You will be pleased to refer to that part of my Letter in which the name of ATTICUS is mentioned.† I learn that the book-appetite of this gentleman is of the same cormorant-capacity as ever : nay, that a return to his native land has rather sharpened than subdued it—that Charles Lewis has been obliged to lay in such a stock of russia and morocco skins—to bind only his black-letter romances in the Italian, Spanish, French and English languages—as may appear incredible to those not having ocular demonstration of its truth. Such a set of tools also has been manufactured for the binding of them, as is altogether marvellous ; and as to the *extent* of his library, to save trouble, you had better say, at once, that it reaches from * * * * * * to Nuremberg ! For proof of an *intermediate* link in a chain of such extension, stop at the *Rue* ———— not a stone's throw from the *Quai Voltaire*—and casting your

* Vol. I. p. xi.   † Page 37.

eye up at a huge mansion, in which 30,000 tomes are deposited—and which has been recently called " *Grand Hôtel Bibliomanesque* "—learn, that,

What was *Bullard's* once, is * * * * *'s now.

But if the days of youth with Atticus are over, his early example has found more than one imitator. Look back also, Reverend Sir, and see if the name of Euphormio, and mention of his meditated book-pyramid,* be easily to be found. When a lad at Eton, I learn that this Euphormio was always "strange and prying," like Henry Dyson of old,† into book-recesses which were but little haunted ; and that an uncut copy of the *Lac Puerorum*, printed by William Faques, or Andrew Skot, first caught his eye and fixed his affections. Those affections have been steady as the polar star, ever since; and now, midway 'twixt his twentieth and thirtieth year, he lords it, without controul, over such a domain of books —in the hall of his ancestors— as would induce an ordinary man to distrust the evidence of his senses. But Euphormio is something, and a good deal, more than a mere Collector of costly and precious volumes. He is a *Bibliographer*, of no common calibre ; and volunteers a world of labour in the specification of the worth and rarity of his several treasures. He is meditating such

* Page 23. † *Bibliomania*, p. 398.

a *Catalogue Raisonné* of these treasures, as may astound even yourself. These be glorious examples to the young—and ought to excite the rivalry of half the Country *Squires* and *Sheriffs* throughout Great Britain.

Nor are other examples wanting of bibliomaniacal ardour in early manhood. I have mentioned the name of MARCUS, as one entitled to no ordinary respect ; and have surmised that, when the trammels of non-age are cut away, the said Marcus will spring at once into distinction among the Collectors of a first-rate class of books. The future will, I am persuaded, prove the truth of this prediction. Again—behold the heir apparent of a *Ducal Coronet*, sedulously sitting down to master volumes, of which his school fellows, and perhaps University comrades, had never heard even the titles. While others are coated in red garments, scouring the plain, or leaping the fence, in pursuit of Reynard's brush— while as many more, or double the number, are levelling the tube of death, and the " whirring pheasant " drops lifeless into the brake— behold our young Bibliomane seated tranquilly in his study, with the *Treasures* of the Greek and Latin languages before him : now reading, now digesting, now writing, and now indulging high thoughts, and brave resolves, touching his future destiny in life. His morning *tiffin* is,

alternately, Aelian and Thomas Magister: his
pétit souper, Porphyrius and Terentianus Maurus:
while of Sidonius Apollinaris, Manilius, and Mercurius Trismegistus, he has sundry little pocket
editions, wherewith he delights himself as he wan-
ders along the butter-cupped meadows. O rare
and felicitous combination of mental labour and
mental recreation! O example, greatly to be
admired—and deserving of imitation, especially
among those whose wealth and situation are at
once great and influential!

But, whatever may be the result of the ducal
heir, we have, in the example of a DUKE himself,
no common illustration of the steadiness and spirit with which an early attachment to Books has
been followed up. To the other, almost innume-
rable, attractions of Chatsworth, look at its *Library:* the beauty of the room, and the yet greater beauty of its furniture! If the Libraries of
the Houses in London, Chiswick, and Chatsworth, be put together, they will not easily be
surpassed by the similar treasures of any mansion,
however lordly and however vast. To books
(of which the purchase of the celebrated library
of the late Bishop of Ely might only be considered as a *graft* on the original stock) add Pictures, Statues, and GEMS .... and you have the most
glorious frame work in which a living portrait
can be encadred! Nor are such treasures idly

dormant in their several receptacles. When *St. Ethelwold* makes his appearance,* it will be seen to what good and useful purposes antiquarian volumes may be devoted. I anticipate a general stir on the occasion, in the upper book-circles, equal to that on the arrival of an ambassador from Persia among the fashionable corps — whose " many twinkling feet " produce such a fevered atmosphere at Almack's.

But there is yet a prouder boast to record. The genuine bibliomaniacal blood is now running at high tide in ROYAL VEINS; and no marvel. Who, that has paced the LIBRARY of GEORGE III, now deposited in the British Museum, has not been well-nigh " dumb-founded " at the glorious visto of interminable book-treasures before him? What Englishman, on such a visit, has not been astonished that these books were the collection of *one man*—and that man, the MONARCH OF HIS COUNTRY!! Can it be a matter of surprise, then, that the mantle of the parent should have descended upon the shoulders of at

---

* The very amiable and accomplished Mr. John Gage is at present occupied in making this " appearance " effective. Mention of this most curious and ancient volume is made in the *Bibliographical Decameron*, vol. I. pp. lv.-lxiii.: but shortly, under the patronage of the Antiquarian Society, (here wisely exerted) all its charms and all its worth will be made palpable to the public gaze. M. R.

least ONE of his sons? You will instantly catch
my allusion; and already we are arm-in-arm
exploring within the elongated library in Kensington Palace. Lately, great acquisitions, in
apartments as well as in books, have added to
the comforts of the Royal Inmate; and a noble
room, just completed, forms a sort of *Lago Mag-
giore,* into which the contents of the neighbouring corridors and boudoirs (crammed with lore of
every philological description!) empty themselves
as tributary streamlets. Nor has His Royal
Highness less ground of receiving congratulation
upon another score. His *Biblical Treasures* have
been laid before the world in the sumptuous Catalogue of them put forth by Mr. Pettigrew,*
adorned with fac similes, and abounding in curious as well as correct intelligence. Such a

---

* BIBLIOTHECA SUSSEXIANA : *A Descriptive Catalogue,
accompanied by historical and biographical notices of the MSS.
and printed books contained in the Library of* H. R. H. the
DUKE OF SUSSEX, &c. in Kensington Palace, 1827, 2 vols.
Impl. 8vo. The first volume is devoted to the MSS.—the
second to the printed books,—in Theology only. Mr. Pettigrew computes the number of *manuscript* volumes in the library
to be 12,000 : of *printed* books, 38,000—five years ago! The
fac simile of the ornaments in some of the Hebrew MSS. are
exceedingly beautiful—and many of them of a very ancient
date. Nothing has been spared in decorative attraction of
paper and printing to render this work in all respects deserving
of the PATRONAGE under which it was given to the world.
CATO PARVUS.

monument of the good taste and gallant spirit of
the OWNER of these treasures, is deserving of all
praise, and is at once splendid and imperishable.
I am not solitary in the expression of a fervent
wish that the Author of this *opus magnum* may
find encouragement to resume his promised labours of continuance. At present, the department of *Theology* (in which the greater and les-
ser Polyglots cut a most distinguished figure)
only is executed.

But it is time, Reverend Sir, to bid you adieu:
and I do so, with the frank avowal that the recollection of all the WORTHIES, here recorded,
puts me into a genial flow of spirits, and more than
counterbalances the dejection which I felt on taking up my pen to address you. In some measure I believe this must be attributed to the sight
of an elegantly got up volume, being an English
version of the *Cynogeticon*, or Book of Hunting,
by ARRIAN, which has been sent down to me
from London since I commenced this Epistle.
The translator is anonymous; but he is clearly an
intelligent, learned, and tasteful man; and I
would rather see this volume upon my table,
than witness the longest *burst* that ever was recorded in the *cynogetical* annals of Leicester-
shire. The book is absolutely a "dear delight,"
and may be consulted again and again with in-

struction and entertainment. Like a *true* Biblio-
maniac, the author printed but a *limited* number
of copies.* But a truce to this rambling. Gravely
and honestly speaking, I would hope that the
examples of bibliomaniacal eminence just brought
forward, may have a beneficial effect in the long
run. Men will in time become tired of the insipi-
dity, fickleness, or worthlessness, of those pursuits,
which leave behind neither tangible nor visible
proofs of their worth. The *Turf* cannot always
be *soft* to its frequenter's foot. The dice-box
cannot always disgorge its *doublets of sixes.* The
bagnio may conceal the *accomplice* as well as the
victim of seduction. Tavern orgies tear asunder
the stoutest constitution, as well as impoverish the
weightiest purses . . . . . . Jaded and distracted in
these exhausting pursuits, the votary of them re-
turns to his private haunt—of loneliness, discomfort, and vexation of spirit! He sees no object to
cheer him—he hears no friendly voice of sympathy—his pillow is stuffed with thorns, and he is
" tossed to and fro" 'midst the snatches of doubt-
ful slumber which that pillow may induce. Where
are the dicta of Epictetus, or the morals of Seneca?
the golden opinions of Antoninus, or the poesy of

* I believe only 250. It is sold by Messrs. Bohn and Son,
and will I hope be out of print before the next November
coursing begins. The embellishments are sweetly appropriate.

Prudentius? Every shelf is bereft of books—
and it is not *here* that we must expect the IN-
SPIRED WORD of heaven! I will not draw the
converse of such a picture. It may be *inferred*
from what has preceded it.

Let the honest trader, therefore, in BOOK MER-
CHANDISE, cheer up his spirits; and if his heart
do not beat quite so high as it hath been wont to
beat, let him be assured that better and brighter
days are at hand. Let the illustrious *subhastalian*
Corps—Messrs. Evans, Sotheby, Wheatley, and
Hodgson—take good courage, and polish up their
ebon-truncheons for a prosperous Spring cam-
paign. Above all, let my old and learned friend,
W. Y. Otley, Esq. no longer hesitate to bring his
Costerian labours before the anxious eyes of the
public.* He will reap a more abundant harvest,
in *every* sense of the word, than he at present may
dare to anticipate. Let the word RE-ACTION
be inscribed over his inner porch; and for those,
who are watching the ebbing and flowing of
chances—who are reluctant to untie their closely

---

* This book, to my *certain* knowledge, will be equally a
curosity and a treasure in its way. Old LAURENCE COSTER
never before had such honor paid him ; and Haerlem has found
in Mr. Otley a champion which may almost justify her forget-
fulness of Meerman. The volume, which will be in 8vo., is
crowded with embellishments, both as fac-similes and illustrations. M. R.

knotted purses—who freeze or burn as a few shillings preponderate—for such, my motto is " now or never!" But, " I have done."*

Claudite jam rivos pueri, sat prata bibêrunt.†

I am always,

Reverend Sir,

Your " Constant Reader,"

And devoted Servant,

Mercurius Rusticus.

---

* Cicero, passim.　　　　　† Virgil, Eclog. iii. v. 111.

For EU product safety concerns, contact us at Calle de José Abascal, 56–1°, 28003 Madrid, Spain or eugpsr@cambridge.org.

www.ingramcontent.com/pod-product-compliance
Ingram Content Group UK Ltd.
Pitfield, Milton Keynes, MK11 3LW, UK
UKHW020325140625
459647UK00018B/2008